MW01078994

THE
ULTIMATE
SURVIVOR

THE INCREDIBLE STORY OF
WALLY PIESZKA,
A MAN WHO WORE THE UNIFORMS
OF BOTH NAZI GERMANY
AND THE ALLIED FORCES,
AND WHO SURVIVED THE
TOUGHEST CHALLENGES
OF THE TWENTIETH CENTURY

J. DENNIS MAREK

THE ULTIMATE SURVIVOR

COPYRIGHT 2017 © J. DENNIS MAREK

1 DEARBORN SQUARE, KANKAKEE, IL 60901

J. Dennis Marek has been a trial lawyer for the last 47 years. He was educated at DePauw University, Durham, University, England, and did his law work at Northwestern University. He formerly worked for the CIA and was an officer in the United States Air Force. He has been a columnist for the *Daily Journal* in Kankakee, Illinois, for the last eight years. He was elected to the American College of Trial Lawyers in 1991. He lives on a farm near Chebanse, Illinois, with his wife, Cathy.

All rights reserved. No part of this publication may be reproduced, stored in a retrieval system, or transmitted, in any form or by any means, electronic, mechanical, photocopying, recording or otherwise, without prior written permission of the publisher, except for brief quotations in critical reviews and articles.

First Edition, October 15, 2017

Printed in the United States
of America

CHAPTERS

ACKNOWLEDGMENTS

How do you write your first book? The primary need is a story. Wally Pieszka gave me that as soon as I met him in 2011. I knew he had a story to tell and one that needed telling. I was a columnist, not a writer of a book. The story was as compelling as Mr. Zamperini's in *Unbroken*. So I wrote to Laura Hillenbrand saying I had a perfect follow-up book for her. She was so ill, she wasn't writing. Then through a fraternity brother, a former fighter pilot and one of the hostages in Iran, Dave Roeder, I was put in touch with author Mark Bowden, of *Blackhawk Down* fame. I asked him to write it.

Mark called me and explained that he was too committed to do the book, but he spent almost an hour on the phone convincing me that I could do it, and he gave me some hints on how. Another person who convinced me to write this book was Sharon Wells Wagner, a publisher and author who had read one of my columns and emailed me. She encouraged me to try.

If it weren't for Rob Small, the owner of the *Daily Journal* in Kankakee, Illinois, who convinced me in 2009 to write a weekly column in his newspaper, my writing career would not have begun. I was already 66 years old. His editor, Phil Angelo, taught me how to write a better column and what not to do or say.

Then there were the readers of the transcripts: Dr. Phil Hays, both my and Wally's doctor; *Daily Journal* editor Tim Yonke; columnist and author Jack Klasey; my law partner, John Coghlan; and my tenacious sisters, Diane Yerkes and Lori Birtley. I learned so much from author Jim Ridings, as well. He edited my drafts, taught me how to copyright, how to self-publish, what to use for photographs, and the ins and outs of making a bunch of type-written pages into a book. A special thanks to Brian Marcotte who not only created the cover, but helped me find my way through computer programs and other areas of which I had little knowledge or ability.

I thank my two secretaries, Barbara Blake and Tami Wagner, along with my receptionist, Lora Boudreau, who helped me with typing and copying, while covering for me at times while I wrote.

Wally's son, Wally Jr., was irreplaceable, as he had heard so many of his father's recollections over the years and could relate some with more detail. He was also a student of Stalingrad, and helped me with facts and details. I want to thank the Kadzielnik family in Ilownica, Poland, for their hospitality when my wife and I visited them in Wally's birth village. They took the time to show us the areas of which Wally spoke, and gave us a feeling of what it might have been like so many years ago in those trying times.

But most of all, I thank my wife, Cathy, who put up with the late suppers when I visited Wally, who sat at night while I wrote, and who read the transcript so many times, each time finding an error or repeat, or a part that made sense to no one but me. Without her patience and help, I would never have had the time to write a story that should be told.

PREFACE

Being forced into manhood while still a boy is not something one foresees when growing up. This is the true story of a man who wore the uniform of Nazi Germany and the uniform of the Allied Forces in World War II; a man forced to work at Auschwitz during its years of horror; a soldier who fought in the bloodiest battle in the history of warfare; an immigrant who came to America and became a confidant of P.K. Wrigley. This is a tale, not only of bravery, but of the determination to survive.

Wladyskaw Pieszka, or Wally as he became known, was born between the wars in a country that knew no peace. Poland was the "taken" land, taken by the Austrians, taken by the Germans, and then taken by the Soviets. All these changes would occur within the life of one man.

Erich Remarque, the German author and World War I veteran, once wrote upon his return home, "Now if we go back we will be weary, broken, burnt out, rootless, and without hope. We will not be able to find our way anymore.... Let the months and years come, they bring me nothing, they can bring me nothing. I am so alone and so without hope that I can confront them without fear."

Wally Pieszka, through determination and fortitude, overcame those words and all of that which should have broken him. Determined to break out of the German imposed authority, Pieszka braved all in the hope that one day he would fight to win back his country and his freedom.

Wally Pieszka is a Polish man and an American; a man with more lives than the proverbial cat. His story would be unbelievable, but for the pictures, records, and documents that authenticate this fabled life. Here is the life of someone who actually wore two uniforms, those of the Axis and the Allies.

Wally's story must begin well before his birth. To even attempt to understand the life the Pieszka family lived in the twentieth century, one must journey back to the early 1900s and what life in Poland was like at the start of World War I. The Great War left eighteen million dead. It brought about change that was unthinkable a few years before. It destroyed the great European empires and left new countries with weak borders. It gave the soldier war machines that were as changed as the invention of gun powder. It led to mass deaths and massacres. It led to ideological dictators who could unite a country into doing unthinkable acts. Here one begins to understand the toll on the family into which he was born.

Some of Wally's war years have gaps of memory. As this book is being written, Wally is 94 years old. Some names and events have faded, but much of his incredible life is retold here in amazingly accurate detail. No stories were embellished. If he didn't remember it, it does not appear.

CHAPTER 1

STALINGRAD

December 17, 1942, 10 p.m. The German Army Private stared at the clear sky in wonder. Could it get any colder? Could he get any hungrier? Could he survive another day? Would he freeze to death tonight? He had taken clothing from dead men for days in his desperate attempts to stay warm. Would tonight be the night that someone would take his?

The quiet was deceiving. The Russian Army was just a few hundred meters away. The Private was standing about ten miles west of Stalingrad, the battle line of the Russian and the German armies. He had been on duty for hours. It was 30 below zero Fahrenheit. He was not dressed for this kind of cold. He wore three shirts and two coats that had not been his only days before, but he was still freezing and he was still starving.

His rations since September had been dramatically reduced. Food had been scarce for the last three months. He was now getting a single cup of cooked wheat bran once a day. It was hardly enough for any man, let alone a soldier fighting a war and sleeping in a hole in the ground. His muscles cried for more in an effort to survive this hell. His body was literally eating itself away. He had lost two dozen pounds fighting this war.

Every part of his body itched. The lice had been with him since September, and he had no salve or medicine to counteract them. He hadn't had a uniform change in three months.

The situation for the soldiers inside the *Kessel* (kettle, or cauldron in English), the name for the encirclement of German troops, was desperate. The Private had been near Stalingrad since September, following a minimal two weeks of training in Germany after being drafted. He had traveled by cattle car to the Ukraine, and then walked six weeks to reach Stalingrad.

The Private was Polish, not German. What was he doing fighting this battle? He had been forced into military service by the threat of death to himself and to his family. Surrounded by German soldiers, he spoke very little German and survived by mimicking what the other soldiers did. While his uniform was the same, his poor German betrayed his true nationality. He was treated with little respect by those who knew his nationality was something other than pure German.

1

Surrounded by Russian forces for the last several weeks, the Sixth Army had been cut off from ground supply. Arms, ammunition, uniforms and food were limited to the supplies that could be flown in by airplane. Two small air strips were still available, but the planes were constantly attacked by Russian fighters. General Friedrich Paulus, the Commander of the Sixth Army, had called for 500 tons of supplies a week, an amount that would barely support the German fighting force assembled in this Russian hell hole. The actual amount being delivered was at best 150 tons a week and sometimes less.

The entire German army was trapped. Their allies to the northwest, the Romanians, had been overrun, as had the Italian forces to the north of the main concentration of German troops.

The time for retreat to the west or south had passed. Gen. Paulus had suggested to Hitler several ways for the embedded German troops to escape, but the Fuehrer had forbidden a retreat or surrender. He could not accept that his war plans were being stopped by a bunch of Russian peasants.

Hitler's ego was becoming the single biggest obstacle to the survival of the Sixth Army. For more than six weeks, Gen. Paulus had been pleading for a withdrawal from the Volga River to save at least some of his troops, but permission never came from Hitler's command post located safely inside Germany. The Fuehrer's orders were simply to stand and defend. Paulus knew it was suicide, but as a good German officer, he obeyed his orders all through the horrific month of December, 1942.

At 19 years of age, the Private had been drafted, and now he was here, shipped to this freezing hell. He had never fired a gun before those two weeks of minimal training. Now he was fighting in the bloodiest battle in the history of warfare.

Stalingrad! The Soviet city was in shambles. Russian civilians were fighting for their lives. Their homes were gone and most had fled to the eastern side of the river. Some remained in the broken buildings and were fighting back. Hundreds of thousands of Soviet and Axis troops had been killed.

The civilian deaths would approach a million before the siege was over. They had died from bombs, fires, gun shots, artillery or just starvation and cold. Before the battle was over in early 1943, the city of Stalingrad would be 95 percent destroyed.

The fate of the army was becoming all too clear to the foot soldiers, as well as to Gen. Paulus and his staff. Almost to the man, the soldiers suffered frozen limbs, filthy uniforms and inadequate winter clothing. They were so weakened that they could hardly move, let alone defend their positions. Morale was virtually nonexistent. That was why the Romanians had been overrun -- they just quit.

The Private was constantly itching in every part of his emaciated body. He had had enough. If only there was a clean, dry uniform, a bath or even a chemical to rid him of the constant itch.

He stood his post, but he did not want to shoot anyone. He had no enemies in this fight. Every day, the Private had to pretend he was a "good German soldier" or he would be shot. He once saw Gen. Paulus in person and heard a soldier ask the commander for more food. The general's only response was that he was starving as well.

Tonight as he stood on watch, the Private spoke aloud as a statement to the entire world. "Moj kochany Boze. Zmiluj sie na demna. Zabiesz mie." ("My dear God. Have mercy on me. Please take me.")

These were the desperate words uttered by the half-frozen man. To speak Polish was forbidden, but he no longer cared. It didn't matter that it was aloud, as no one was near. The Private debated deserting his post. That night he no longer cared about life; not his nor anyone else's. His extra-long shift was ordered by the sergeant because he was not a pure German soldier. He had already stood his watch. He then walked away from his post, a capital offense.

The Private walked several hundred meters over the frozen dirt and debris to a hole in the ground covered with boards and branches. This was his "barracks." Inside, it had dirt walls and floor, and it offered shelter from the wind, and was at least a few degrees warmer from the body heat given off by the five fellow soldiers already inside.

As he entered, the Private was confronted by his Sergeant. It was clear that he had left his assigned post.

"You will return to your post," he was told. He stalled for a few minutes. While he understood the order, he did not have the German words to successfully argue with the sergeant. The increase of only a few degrees in temperature and being out of the wind brought an immense relief. He was unsure what to do; if he refused to return to his position, he would be shot. Soldiers by the dozens were being shot by their own officers and non-coms for desertion or merely refusing to obey an order. Chaos ran rampant in the ranks.

The Private wavered. Die here or to freeze to death outside? Which one? Did it really matter? Death was death. It might just be a relief.

Every human reaches a point where death seems the simpler answer. He finally decided that his fate was in his hands. He chose to live, perhaps only for a few more hours or days, but he was going to try to live.

Slowly, the Private climbed back out of the dugout and began walking back to his post. He wouldn't be relieved until 5 in the morning. He thought about 5 a.m., and an old saying flashed in his head. "5 a.m., the time when drunken men start to sweat and the other men start to have nightmares." Well, he wasn't drunk and there was no chance he would sweat, but he was about to have more nightmares, that much he believed.

He had gone only fifteen or twenty meters from the hut when he heard the roar of incoming fire. The sky lit up next to him. The explosion rocked him. Russian artillery had dropped a single shell right into the dugout. All five of the men he had left only minutes ago, including the sergeant, were killed.

He really hadn't known any of them very well. They were all German and he was the odd Polish-German soldier. There was no respect given any of the foreign soldiers conscripted by force into the German Army. The foreigners were just more cannon fodder for the German war machine.

The Private had seen so many die, including a Polish man he had known from home who died in his arms just a few weeks before.

Previously, bullets hit his helmet on two occasions, leaving him with ringing ears and a headache, but no damage.

Once, a bullet passed over his shoulder so closely that it burned his skin. This time, the Private was seriously injured.

His mind was fast becoming as numb as his feet. The last thing he remembered was the roar of the explosion and a searing pain in his right knee. He collapsed and fell unconscious into a ditch that was deep with snow.

For the Private, this wound became the first major event in his series of incredible survivals over the next 14 years.

Whether watched over by God, or if he was the most determined man, or the luckiest man in the world, this Private's survivability would continue for more than seven decades. His lifetime of ordeals was just getting started. Was he to become the luckiest or the unluckiest of men? Time would tell.

This is the story of that lucky/unlucky, boy/man, Private Wladyslaw Pieszka.

CHAPTER 2

POLAND, BEFORE AND AFTER THE GREAT WAR

Many people today have little real understanding of the Great War, later to be called World War I, since there was to be a second and even more deadly worldwide conflict a few short years later. But to understand Wally's ancestors, their mindsets, their culture, and their basic struggle for mere survival, one must first look to their history.

The Polish people were intimately involved with that first major world conflict. It affected almost every facet of their daily lives and also affected the borders of their country. Poland did not exist geographically at the beginning of World War I in 1914. As a country, it had not "existed" for 120 years. Its various parts had been stolen by the Austrians, the Russians and the Germans.

Poland was doomed over the centuries to be the battleground of Eastern Europe because of the competing interests of those who wanted to feed their people from the wheat fields of this prolific country. There were innumerable battles to control this fertile land and the Polish people whose skills produced mammoth crops.

In the early 13th century, the Teutonic Knights attacked Poland from Germany. The town of Danzig had resisted, so the Knights retaliated. They killed more than ten thousand citizens and replaced them with German immigrants. Pleas from Poland for assistance in their struggle went in vain. Perhaps it was confusion in communications. In those days, most Polish places had two names. Gdnask was Danzig, Szczecion was also Stettin, and even the river Wisla was called the Vistula. No one came to the aid of the Polish. Perhaps none of the bordering areas even cared.

A familiar phrase repeated over the years in Poland is, "A Pole is a man born with a sword in his right hand, and a brick in his left. When the battle is over, he starts to rebuild." After each war, Poland, the breadbasket of the central European states, would rebuild.

The Poles farmed. They had few factories or larger business concerns. Thus, they were often considered lacking in intelligence and useful skills off the farm. They toiled under a feudal system, which forced them to bargain for prices, but they most often lacked the skills to market their own produce.

After the Teutonic Knights came the Tatars (Mongols), who raped their women and pillaged their land in the 14th century. These invaders often killed the men or took them as slaves. Again and again, Poland was overrun, enslaved and controlled by neighboring foreign powers.

Borders changed like the seasons. As a result, it was impossible for people in these conditions to learn government and how to run their own country. It was almost impossible to even know what constituted the country. After so many wars, the period just before World War I found Poland a most confusing patchwork of various parts. Russia held an eastern portion; the Germans, a western area; and Austria-Hungary controlled the central and southern areas. Each part was pushed up against the others. Krakow was technically in Austria-Hungary, while other Polish cities and villages were controlled by Germany or Russia. Silesia now had more German-speaking inhabitants than any other group.

Wally Pieszka's mother's family had lived for many years in an Austrian-controlled area in the rural countryside of what was originally southwest Poland. Under Austrian rule, the people spoke Polish, sang Polish songs, and wandered down streets with Polish names on the signs. While technically there was no Poland, these were people who felt themselves to be Polish.

The Austrians, prior to World War I, believed they needed a strong army to defend their lengthy borders. They drafted from every corner of their controlled Empire. The Austrian Army spoke almost a dozen languages, among them Czech, Slovak, Serbian, Slovene, Ruthenian, Polish, Italian, Hungarian and German.

For several years before World War I, Count Andrez Lubonski, based in Vienna, was in charge of the Polish areas of the Austrian Empire. While he had Polish roots, Lubonski had to conform to the Austrian ways as he directed the control of this subdued country.

In this southwest corner of what used to be Poland, was the village of Skoczow, near the larger town of Bielsko-Biala. It was here that the pre-World War I Polish people tried to maintain a country and a culture.

At the end of the war, the victorious allies gave Poland back to its people. The parts that had been stolen by the Russians, the Germans and the Austrians were reassembled. Lubonski, at the age of 68, left his beautiful Viennese palace and traveled to his family home near Gorka. He became a self-appointed principal advisor to the newly formed nation of Poland. Lubonski spent a great deal of time in Warsaw, the recognized capital of the reformed country. He helped transform this new country into a conjoined monarch. By 1939, however, Poland would once again cease to be its own country.

During those brief years between 1918 and 1939, Poland faced numerous political problems. The largest problem the new government encountered in 1918 was the existence of substantial non-Polish minorities inside the new borders, with each group desiring some sort of independent power.

Recent history convinced the controlling government that strong alliances were necessary for growth and continued safety. Count Lubonski sought an alliance with the Ukrainians, knowing that training these former Cossacks to govern themselves would bring a time when they would seek their own government. He faced a similar concern for any relationship with Lithuania.

This dilemma showed itself in numerous areas where there were attempts to unite heterogeneous groups into a single country and culture. These newly formed countries would seek a certain independence that would not serve them well in the coming years, but that was deemed, by their leader, to be far off in time.

In the western portion of the new Poland was an area ceded to it by the Versailles Treaty. This former German area was known as Silesia. Its substantial German population was not at all happy with its role in this new country again called Poland.

To the south, similar issues were raised by the Czechoslovaks. Borders were not always rivers or mountains but merely lines drawn on a map proclaiming an area where many inhabitants didn't know the principal language or its customs. All this led to disputes and varying alliances as Polish neighbors began to reclaim their military power.

Another ethnic problem was the substantial number of Jews. Prior to the 1700s, Poland had welcomed Jewish immigrants from other countries where their persecutors had run rampant. In this new period of Polish independence, however, some of the old religious prejudices resurfaced.

While the rest of the new country was celebrating and enjoying the independence, many of these fortunate, but poor, Jews were not aligned with this new wave of freedom and were doubtful of any continuing safety. The two groups were suspicious of each other during this brief twenty-one years of Polish independence.

This was the setting where a young Polish man and woman met in 1907 and married the following year. Their life seemed settled into the typically rural Polish family tradition. A home was their first consideration, followed by having their own family.

Such was not to be the intended course for this young couple.

CHAPTER 3

THE KADZIELNIKS

Sophia Holksa, the woman who would become Wally Pieszka's mother, was born in 1884 into a family of 14 children in the Polish village of Ilownica.

A family of that size was not all that unusual. Twelve of the fourteen children survived infancy, and the family shared a home consisting of only two and a half rooms. All the boys slept in one bed and the girls in another. Her parents slept in the great room that also comprised the kitchen and living area.

Sophia attended four years of school before working full time on the family farm. Such was the extent of education expected of rural Polish youth, especially a girl.

Andrew Kadzielnik was born in Bzenna, three villages away, in 1888. By comparison, his family was small; he had only two sisters and no brothers. Andrew received an education similar to Sophia's before becoming a full-time worker on his family farm.

Sophia and Andrew met at a village dance in 1907 and married in 1908. Poland was under Austrian control as part of the Hapsburg Empire. It had almost no economy of its own other than agriculture. Farming was the predominant source of employment and income. Money could not be borrowed from banks. Jobs were scarce.

Andrew was determined to build a place for his new wife. Slowly, he and Sophia began construction of a home but it took years to complete. Meanwhile, they lived in the farm home of her parents.

The world was at peace for a while after Sophia and Andrew wed. The young couple soon started their family. Frank was born in 1909, and Emil followed in 1912. Their home was finally completed in 1912 and the family was able to move in.

Unbeknownst to the young couple, war was only months away. The European royal families had intermarried for years, but symbolic relationships were no more binding on lasting peace than royal courtships or marriages. Peaceful diplomacy was almost non-existent. Political leaders were steeped in military training, and peace was only thought to be accomplished with a larger army. Therefore, the strength of armies far outweighed any leaders trained in diplomacy. Attempts at working out peaceful solutions to international problems were unheard of. Military might was all that mattered.

In the summer of 1914, military maneuvers were held in Bosnia, which had been annexed into the Austrian Empire in 1908. Archduke Franz Ferdinand, the nephew of Emperor Franz Joseph and heir to the Austrian throne, arrived in Bosnia to supervise the army on June 25, 1914.

With the training maneuvers concluded, the Archduke and his wife motored north to the provincial capital of Sarajevo to carry out more official duties there. The 28th of June was an ill-chosen day for such a visit, because this day marked the anniversary of the defeat of Serbia by the Turks in 1389. Called Vidov Dan, it was the date on which Serbia commenced suffering nothing but a long history of foreign oppression. The Serbs felt that the Austrian Hapsburgs were a continuation of this oppression. Franz Ferdinand was warned that his presence was unwelcome and might be dangerous. He ignored the warnings.

A team of five young Serbs and a Muslim Bosnian attempted a bombing of Franz Ferdinand's car, but the bomb bounced off its hood. The car drove safely off, but later made a wrong turn and ended up in front of one of the conspirators who had not been captured. Gavrilo Princip, armed with only a revolver, stepped forward and fired repeatedly. The Archduke's wife died instantly. The Archduke died a few minutes later.

A totally unnecessary war started shortly thereafter to soothe the egos of certain leaders, which became the Great War. Soon, three continents would be engaged in the largest war the world had ever seen.

Andrew Kadzielnik was to be one of the millions of pawns in this great exchange of egos of national leaders.

Andrew was taken from his pregnant wife and two young sons when he was drafted in early March 1914. After leaving his family and their new farmhouse, he received minimal military training, then was shipped east to face the Russian forces opposing Austria and its Empire.

He was just one of the cogs in the great Austrian war machine. Andrew was dead by August, killed by Russian forces in his first major confrontation near the Ukraine border. Andrew would never see his third son, who was born in September, a month after his death. The boy was named Andrew for his dead father.

Sophia Kadzielnik inherited the small farm and the house, numbered 123, from her deceased husband. As the war raged on for four more long years, life was almost impossible for this young widow with three young boys. Although Sophia received a very small military pension for the death of her husband, it was not enough for the survival of her family.

Livestock and grain harvested from the farm were the only food sources and income for this family of four. Sophia was the only adult who could tend to all the chores. The labor to plant and harvest the crops, care for the few animals, milk the cow, and at the same time maintain a home for her family and raise three boys was no less than an Herculean task.

A year into this grueling life, a further tragedy struck. Toward the end of 1915, Sophia and the children lost their house to a fire that probably started in the kitchen. While all escaped, their home was a total loss. Accidental burning of homes was not uncommon, as heating, though minimal, was almost always done with open fires in stoves and fireplaces.

The family farm was small, only four hectares, and could barely supply an existence for this family, let alone provide extra funds to rebuild a home. There was no money and no male labor. Who would loan money to a poor widow with a destitute family?

Not only was the house gone, every worldly possession of the family was gone. Only the clothes the family was wearing remained. Fortunately, the livestock survived, but the food supply that had been carefully harvested and stored in the cellar had been destroyed.

Sophia had no options. The meager pension would not house or feed her family. Her hardest efforts could not provide shelter. Utter desperation set in on this woman of 31, and her children ages 6, 3 and 1.

Yet, hers was not the sole wartime tragedy in the small town of Ilownica. Widows abounded as a result of the Austrian draft and the battles with the Russians. There were so many tragedies that daily life went on with minimal sympathy.

Such were the times. There was time for crying only at night as an exhausted Sophia lay down.

CHAPTER 4

END OF THE GREAT WAR

Finally, the heartbreaking war ended with the peace accords signed June 28, 1919. The Paris Peace Conference decided the fate of Germany and her allies, but Germany and Austria were not permitted to attend.

Three distinct conditions imposed by that Treaty would cause German hatred for the next twenty years and would be a significant factor in the rise of Adolph Hitler.

The first edict was the stripping away of massive amounts of land from Germany. More than 25,000 square miles of land were ceded to other countries. As a result, 700,000 people would no longer live in Germany.

Most of Upper Silesia went to Poland, along with two territories known as Posen and Pomerania. The latter gave Poland its only link to the sea, known as the Polish Corridor. While the majority of Poles were farmers, this port was their only link to the seas for exportation of grain, and some fishing. The rest of Upper Silesia was to have a plebiscite to decide its country of citizenship. In other words, these people had the right to choose their nationality, something unheard of before this time, or since.

The second provision of the Accord was the prohibition of any rearmament by Germany for 20 years. This provision was unanimously agreed upon by all the Allied partners. The third of the provisions, while adopted, was not unanimously supported. Article 123, later known as "The Guilt Clause," proposed payment to other countries of reparations for the damages caused to them (for example, to the French coal industry). The actual costs incurred by the Allies in defending the war were also to be included. Certain British and American leaders felt that this part of the Accord was unfair and humiliating to the loser. It called for payments in excess of 132 billion marks or the equivalent of $31.4 billion in 1919 dollars. This was clearly an impossible task for a defeated country.

Before the war concluded, Sophia Kadzielnik was the talk of the tiny village. She was a war widow with three young sons, but she had no home. Maria Kopec, also a war widow for three years, had two sons of her own. More importantly, she had a home.

Maria, who had known Sophia at school, offered a single room in her house, known merely as #82, to this family of four. The Kopec house was large for the period, and half was reserved for Maria and her boys. The northwest quarter was used by Sophia's family, and the final quarter housed the Kopec cows. Sophia and her three boys' portion measured only 20 by 20 feet, but it was welcome shelter.

Sophia had little choice. There was no way to even attempt to start a new home. Besides the lack of money and ability to borrow the same, Sophia also lacked a male family member (in those times so necessary to contemplate such a large project); her eldest was but seven years of age. She gratefully accepted Maria's offer of a home. While the war raged on, the Kadzielniks had a roof over their heads.

Sophia helped with the cooking and provided some of the food since the Kadzielnik farm was still tilled by her and her oldest boy, Frank, producing some crops. Her cows gave the Kopec household additional milk and butter, and her chickens gave eggs. The surplus milk and eggs could be sold to supplement her small Austrian war pension.

Sophia's quarters were austere and humble. The furniture and household necessities consisted of two beds, a stove, a table, a sink and three chairs. All were contributions from fellow church-goers. There was a small crucifix on the wall next to Sophia's bed, but the remaining walls were bare brick. There was an outhouse behind the home that both families shared.

Work now was even harder with the need to produce more food and eggs in order to share with Maria's family. Maria did not insist that they contribute, but it was the only way to repay Maria for her generosity. Sophia also needed to contribute for her own pride. Fortunately, as the boys grew, the two eldest took a more active part in the farm and livestock work.

As Sophia supported her three boys and shared Maria's house into the 1920s, ill feelings by Germany toward all of its victorious neighbors simmered. It was only a matter of time before that kettle would boil over.

For the Kadzielnik family, survival far outweighed any loftier thoughts about the future. Day after day, Sophia and her young boys struggled for enough to survive. Thoughts of rebuilding were mere idle dreams in the early years after this terrible conflict that took her husband, and ill fortune took her home. The actual ending of the war made little difference to Sophia and her boys, as they had already lost practically everything. They had no more to lose except their lives and their freedom.

Maria and Sophia developed a most unusual relationship. Sophia did not want to take advantage of Maria, even though she knew the gift of a residence by Maria was purely altruistic. Their desires for their children were quite similar. Both women wanted schooling for their boys and insisted that they all attend the local school in Ilownica regularly.

The hope of each mother was for her sons to have a better and more peaceful life than their husbands had. They all attended the Catholic church regularly, listening to the hopeful words of the parish priest.

Four Kadzielniks living in a room just slightly larger than 400 square feet was close to intolerable, but there was no other choice. This young widow felt she was growing old too quickly with little hope of respite. She had little to offer a man. No home, no time, and three boys in need of being raised.

As the years passed her by, she consoled herself with the fact that she was coping and was raising her sons. More than that, she was a Pole, a person determined to meet her obstacles and overcome them.

This trait was not lost on Sophia's sons or on a son who was yet to come. The stoic training by Sophia was to have a profound effect on her children.

CHAPTER 5

FAMILY GROWTH

When time permitted the young widow to take a breath, Sophia occasionally attended dances in her village of Ilownica on Saturday nights, sometimes with Maria. Other than these dances and church each Sunday, there was no social life in a village barely on the positive side of survival.

In 1922, however, fate took a moment to shine on this widow. While at one of the dances, she met a man who had not been called up for the war. He was a railroad conductor, thus a worker in a critical industry. He had avoided being sent to the Russian Front. He did not attend the dances regularly, as his work often kept him away from his home for several days at a time. This often included weekends.

His name was Franciszek Pieszka, and he seemed quite sophisticated to Sophia. While the mother of three was not necessarily a marriage catch, Franciszek danced with her several times the first evening, and on his return three weeks later he asked her out.

The two courted for several months and each knew they had fallen in love. But Sophia could not afford to marry, as this would have voided her Austrian pension as a war widow. The day came, however, that marriage was inevitable. A child was not only on the way but had arrived in the tiny Kadzielnik household.

Wladyslaw (Wally) Pieszka was born on May 23, 1923, prior to the marriage of his parents. This was a bit out of order for the times, but understandable with her issue with her pension.

As good Catholics, a marriage usually took place before the birth. In a small local ceremony, at which the village priest, Stanislov Niemuk, performed the rites, Sophia and Frank were married in Ilownica a few months later.

Once Franciszek Pieszka moved into the Kopec house, there were six people in this confined room. The home was bursting at its seams. There was one bed for Sophia and Franciszek and for a while the only other bed held the three older boys. A bench that was used as infant Wally's bed was also used for eating. Each night Sophia put padding on the bench, pushed it up to the foot of the boys' bed for support, and put a single blanket on it for Wally's bed. He slept on that bench for almost three years.

Oldest son, Frank Kadzielnik, now almost 15, often spent time at the home of one of his mother's sisters, herself a widow, who lived in the next village. He just needed to have room to stretch his legs, but there had been no offer of housing him on a more permanent basis. Each family had to survive on its own. His 12-year-old brother, Emil, eventually followed Frank's lead when the aunt had reached the ability to support these two young nephews.

Wally's early years were spent in and around Maria Kopec's house and his village. Occasionally, his Czech cousin and family would cross the new border just south of Ilownica for visits. There were few boys Wally's age, although Andrew, the youngest of his half-brothers, did spend time with Wally. While this related cousin was Polish by descent, the redistricting of countries following the Versailles Treaty changed their family's home from being inside Poland to Czechoslovakia.

Wally's cousin, just a few months older than he, often ridiculed Wally for being Polish, while he was Czech. At first, Wally did not comprehend the difference being pointed out to him, but he soon tired of the humiliation and found ways to even the score.

This cousin, Francek Holexa, though only slightly older than Wally, spoke Czech in addition to German and Polish. Francek attended a Czech school, but soon transferred to a German one. He was haughty and constantly teasing Wally, calling him the "dirt boy" or "farmer boy." Wally spent hours thinking of ways to get even. It seemed that Francek was becoming that young man that the Nazis were preparing to train as devoted German military officers.

For Francek to speak German was not that unusual. Wally's mother did as well, having been raised in Silesia, an area that contained as many Germans as Poles during the last forty years.

Once, years later and after military training by the Germans, Francek entered the Pieszka home, saluted and shouted, "Heil Hitler." Wally's mother immediately responded in perfect German, "In this house you will greet us with, 'Praise Jesus Christ.'" Francek said nothing and walked out of the house.

While not a bad boy, Wally was clever and he walked the edge of good and not-so-good behavior. He was a very resourceful and creative thinker. One by one, Wally devised tricks to even the score with his haughty cousin. Down by one of the lakes, Wally let it slip that there were mammoth goldfish in the water. "You have to get right next to the water and peer straight down," he informed his cousin. As Francek leaned forward, the pet goat that followed Wally everywhere spotted his target. "Bara. Bara. Boots!" yelled Wally, the signal to the goat to ram straight ahead, this time into the rear of his cousin. Francek went straight into the water. Wally professed ignorance that the goat would do such a thing, but the dripping wet cousin had his doubts. This goat never once butted his buddy, Wally.

On another occasion, Wally invented "Hocus Pocus," calling it black magic. Wally had heard these foreign words from brother, Andrew.

With these new words, Wally conjured up his own magic. Staring openly at a fresh cow dropping, Wally informed his cousin that staring and the use of the magic words could make the cow pie disappear. Francek began staring intently while Wally pulled his cousin's feet from beneath him, having his cousin settle completely on the dropping in his fancy lederhosen. After these two adventures, cousin Francek chose to be more careful with his criticism. His naïveté of the rural Polish pranks also disappeared. Wally felt somewhat justified in his pranks, but after these glorious events, Francek was much too wary to be fooled again.

At the age of six, Wally began his formal Polish education. As a first grader, Wally attended a local school in Ilownica. Andrew attended a different school a few miles away and they always walked at least part way together each morning. Wally's school was not particularly well equipped, but he accepted it as he didn't know what any other school might be like.

Rural Polish schools were quite basic, and were not staffed with trained teachers. In most cases, the teachers in these schools were local women who could read and had started in education by teaching their own children and then gradually were persuaded or chose to help other Polish children. As such they became the teachers. Formal education was considered less important than farming and survival.

Polish life in the country did not yield the luxury of continued education. Schooling in the Catholic religion prompted some attention to a formal education, but as a child became bigger and stronger, survival of the farming family constantly called the growing child back home. The pressing need limited the years of formal education. Wally's life was no different than that of other children.

Francek returned home for his German/Czech education. Visits became less frequent as the lives of these two young men became more polarized. Over time, Wally's cousin became further indoctrinated in Nazism and actually served in the German SS for many years. His language ability and attitude fit the character of what the German military machine wanted.

CHAPTER 6

SCHOOL AND FAMILY HOME

The Pieszka family continued to farm their acreage and tend to the valuable animals that Wally's mother had so carefully protected. Since there were no banks that would loan money to rebuild the farm house, Wally's parents saved and waited.

Farming was not Wally's dream. He saw the shopkeepers and observed how they were independent, and most times they seemed affluent. But, as his mother often pointed out, these shops were almost exclusively owned by Jewish families. Wally's entire family had been Catholic since time began.

Wally's father, with his job as a railroad conductor, was gone for 48 hours at a time, riding trains within Poland from the German border to the Russian border. When they had the time, which wasn't often, and there was some extra money, which was even less often, the family worked on the house. Money was even less available than time.

Construction on the family house started in 1925. It was minimally completed in 1928 when the family moved in. With the completion of their home, the family left the Kopec house after almost thirteen years.

While sharing a home came to an end, Wally and Mrs. Kopec maintained a close relationship for years. Frank and Emil left the Kopec home during the construction period. Frank became a tool and die maker in a neighboring village, while Emil joined the Polish Army in 1927. The family of six was now down to four and had so much more room.

The house had a foundation of poured concrete, but only two rooms were "finished" when the family took up residence. The new home was brick and the interior walls were plastered. While the entire floor was concrete, the stairs to the second story were wooden and made from local lumber hewn from the forest to the north. The first room was a kitchen containing a stove, table and a bed for the boys measuring 10 by 14 feet.

The second was a bedroom for Sophia and Franciszek. There was also a basement and an attic. The basement was a mere 16 feet square, and was constructed for the storage of food, fruit and seeds for next year's crops. An attic was built to hold straw for more insulation. Later, a second bedroom was added. Wally and Andrew were happy to share this new luxurious space.

Their furniture was hand-made in the village. Two old family friends, Florean and Victor Wojnowo, built the chairs, table and wardrobe. The remaining furniture was built by village carpenters.

A village the size of Ilownica, 200 homes at most, could only support so many public works. Wally's elementary school was one such structure. Wally's first class had about twenty-five students and he knew all his classmates.

Each day as he walked to and from school, Wally passed the home of Mrs. Kopec and he thought about the years he had spent there. On occasion, he would stop and visit this lady who had meant so much to him and his family. Mrs. Kopec would never remarry.

Wally felt safe walking in his own village and was learning to enjoy his early schooling and his new freedom. He studied Polish, mathematics, history and geography.

Andrew and Wally started each day walking together for a while, but soon Andrew had to branch off in a different direction. The school had but three teachers for all six grades. In addition, once a week, a priest from the neighboring village gave two hours of religious instruction. This priest later helped Wally make profound decisions about his life.

Since all the students were in small but adjoining classrooms, Wally could often hear the instructions given to the class ahead of him and even tried to do the work. He tried to understand mathematics from the very first time he heard the term, whether in his class or an adjoining one. Wally was quick to learn, but his early experiences were far from intellectual.

Growing up in the Kopec home and working on the farm with his mother and brothers had taught him survival and basic skills, but there were no books in the Pieszka house, save a Bible. Often a child was called back to the farm as soon as he or she was strong enough. His years of schooling would be rather short-lived.

When Wally started third grade, he attended a brand new school building. His old school had outlasted its usefulness. This new school building was modern with a furnace and running water. There was even a shower room with hot water for the students. Since Wally's house did not have such a luxury, he often showered there before coming home.

Schooling in the local village continued for Wally through sixth grade. Life was simple and enjoyable. Eventually, Andrew also left the Pieszka new home to live with the aunt, in the next village, leaving Wally the only child at home.

In the late spring of 1932, at the age of 9, Wally met a girl named Regina Urbach. She was his age and she was very pretty. Regina went to Wally's school, but she went straight home each day after classes. Her father was a shopkeeper, and the Jewish family was considered "well off."

Wally would talk to Regina at school and sometimes walk home with her and her brother, Otto.

Otto and Wally became friends, sharing ideas and comparing religions. When Wally heard that Jews could not eat pork, he managed on occasion to "borrow" some kielbasa from his mother's kitchen. He and Otto would sneak into the forest where Otto ate his first forbidden food. Otto loved this new treat.

Wally continued to accompany Regina home from school until he finally was invited into the Urbach home. It was simple but neat. There was more furniture, and of nicer quality, than that in Wally's house. He met Mrs. Urbach, and although she treated him politely, she seemed cautious. Other women warmed to Wally -- his aunts, even the women in the neighborhood. He was handsome to say the least. But why was Regina's mother so different in her attitude toward Wally, he wondered.

During this time, Wally's mother and his brother, Andrew, encouraged him to become friendly with another local girl, Alos Kieczka. Alos was a Polish Catholic girl and that seemed, as far as the Pieszka/Kadzielnik family was concerned, the right kind of mate for young Wally, even though he was only 10 years old. Unfortunately for his family, Wally found Alos unattractive, spoiled and not very smart. She would never do. Regina had all the qualities he wanted except that her Judaism was a problem for both families.

One day while in the Urbach home, Wally blurted out, "Someday I am going to marry your daughter, Mrs. Urbach."

Mrs. Urbach looked Wally straight into his eyes, "Oh Wally, that is not possible," she replied, but she made no explanation. That evening he repeated to his mother what he had said to Mrs. Urbach.

"You can't, Wally, Regina is Jewish. Jews marry Jews and Catholics marry Catholics," she explained. "And that is just the way it is in Poland."

During much of the school year, daylight was short. The family only had kerosene lamps for lighting. Wally attended school eight hours Monday through Friday, counting the time to walk to and from school. There was also a half day on Saturday. The evening was filled with chores before any homework or dinner. Then it was off to bed.

In early 1938, the Pieszka house was electrified, with a switch on the wall and a light bulb in the middle of the ceiling. There were no wall receptacles, since no one had anything to plug into such an outlet. The family did have a battery operated radio and could listen on occasion to programs broadcast from Krakow.

Upon the completion of sixth grade, Wally again had to change schools. The school in Ilownica only went through grade six. A new school had been built in the neighboring town of Chybie. This new school was a forty-five minute walk from Wally's home. It was spacious and again had showers for the students to use, but Wally was not ready for this next level. Schooling became more difficult. He no longer found it interesting. To the chagrin of his mother, Wally decided to take a year off. He promised his mother that he would return to school the following year.

When Wally was 13, his brother Frank married. The family gathered in full, including the Czech relatives. The wedding was at the local church, but a party followed at the new Pieszka home. The attendees had an ample supply of alcoholic beverages from which to choose. Unbeknownst to his mother, Wally decided for the first time he would participate. At the end of the evening, Andrew found his younger brother on the ground, dead-drunk, and asleep. Unfortunately, his mother also became aware of Wally's condition and there was a lot of extra work around the farm for the next few weeks for this adventurous boy. Wally was coming of age in many ways.

In October of 1936, tragedy struck the Pieszka family. While his father was away, a telegram came to the Pieszka home. There had been an accident on the railroad, and his father had been seriously hurt.

Franciszek Pieszka was in a hospital in Bielsko, about 20 miles from Wally's home. He had fallen under a railcar. His left hand had been run over by a wheel, severing a part of the hand.

Sophia went immediately to the hospital and stayed there for two days. Wally was left alone at home to attend school and fend for himself.

On a second visit to the hospital, Sophia brought Wally. There in the dark hospital room, Wally could see how small the bandaged hand was. He was told that part of the hand was gone. Wally thought of all the things his father could no longer do. Fortunately, their home was completed and Wally was big enough to help with the farm work, but life became a bit more demanding for the 13-year-old.

Franciszek Pieszka lost his job as a result of that accident, but received a pension from the railroad. Unknown to him, in some ways this injury served him well, as he would be no use in the army for any side in the upcoming conflict. Rumors of a rebuilding of Germany and the new Third Reich floated around the community, but rural Polish families had little time for international news. Survival was their day-to-day preoccupation.

As the Polish people rested from a long harvest, and as sons were conscripted into the Polish Army, the world stood on the edge of disaster in November of 1938. Word was out even in Wally's small community that Hitler and Germany were on the move. But people who survived day to day paid little attention to things that they could not change. Poland had been invaded so many times that it might have seemed inevitable that someone would again try to forcefully take the vast productive farm land from the people. Since World War I, Poland had been awarded some former German land as a retribution payment. Germany wanted it back.

November 8, 1938, was a telling night for much of the world, as German hoodlums destroyed Jewish shops throughout Germany in what was called *Kristallnacht*, referred to as the night of the shimmering of the broken glass of Jewish shopkeepers. Poland, as France and many other European countries, still believed that Hitler would not invade their homeland. Let him duke it out with Stalin, they said. The European powers saw the coming war, as did the Polish officials. But it seemed that no matter what British Prime Minister Neville Chamberlain gave to Hitler, he wanted more. Czechoslovakia was to follow Austria, and the move was on. Poland appeared to be next. However, the people of Ilownica remained relatively unaware.

In Britain, Winston Churchill opposed Chamberlain's "peace with honor" speech, which gave away Czechoslovakia, and Churchill was quoted as responding, "You were given the choice between war and dishonor. You chose dishonor, and you will have war." On March 28, 1939, Madrid fell to Franco's armies and the Spanish republic surrendered. Prague had fallen and Poland could not be far behind.

During the same time period, in the fall of 1938, Emil married and came back to the Pieszka home to live with his new wife in a newly created third bedroom. He met his wife while in the Polish Army. Her name also was Sophia. Emil left the military service and was helping on the farm. He also helped with the household expenses and his wife assisted with the cleaning and cooking. This arrangement was to be short-lived, however, as word of possible war with Germany spread, and in early 1939 Emil was drafted back into the Polish forces.

Andrew had already enlisted and was stationed north of Krakow. Emil had to leave his pregnant wife with his mother and family. Another husband leaving a pregnant wife. The irony occurred to Sophia Pieszka.

Wally worked odd jobs, and soon started a most lucrative business selling perfume. Wally had become quite close with his father's sister, Maria Krasnik. Aunt Maria seemed so worldly, and often purchased items from mail order catalogues to resell to others. Wally caught on. He could buy perfume through his aunt, go door-to-door, and sell it to local women for twice the price. Wally's mother would totally have disapproved of such activities. This type of retailing was for the Jews. Therefore, Wally's business dealings were completely between aunt and nephew. It seemed that Wally's aunt was more of a "modern" woman in those times. She even taught him to dance.

The young salesman had perfected a selling approach. Polish people were not accustomed to frequent bathing. Rural woman often smelled of their sweat, and perhaps the cows they fed and milked. Wally would tell the young, available women how his older brothers complained of the way the Polish women smelled. He would tell the women to take sponge baths and then cover those odors with his sweet perfumes. The boys would then love them at the dances.

Wally carried four distinct scents, each one stronger than the last. The women would want to smell each, but Wally would only put a drop on his finger for the test. The product, he claimed, was just too expensive for free samples. He learned how to approach people with a sense of concern and knowledge. This served him well in his perfume sales and other "business" dealings he had with local shopkeepers and their customers.

This rather ingenious business continued until the Germans arrived. Wally was fast learning the tricks of business. He would occasionally share his profits with his mother, but he was careful to always have a pretend story for the extra cash he had accumulated. His mother never learned of his first entrepreneurial venture. Wally was crafty, and all his cunning and persuasive ways were to be soon tested.

Not all experiences in Wally's life were positive. While he often got into trouble in school for pulling the pigtails of the girls in front of him, there were serious events in Polish life. One of his closest friends, also 13, had a job delivering bread for his father's bakery. To do this he took the only family horse. On the way back from a delivery, the horse slipped on the ice and broke its leg. The horse had to be put down, leaving the family with no horse to transport the bakery goods. Two days later, the boy, so distraught with what had happened while he was in charge of the horse, hanged himself in the barn. Wally pondered this act for months, never really understanding the kind of pressure that came with survival of the family. His friend was the first person close to him who died, but he was not to be the last.

During this same period of time, Wally had his own close call with death. One winter day he had decided to cut across the small river to get home a bit faster. As he crossed the ice covered river, he heard a loud crack and the ice gave way. Wally struggled with the freezing water, but he knew how to swim and finally made it to the other shore.

He hurried home to some warmth, but within a few days he was deathly ill. The doctor was summoned and confirmed that Wally had pneumonia. There were no drugs for such a condition at the time, and pneumonia was a leading cause of death in Poland in 1938.

For ten days, Wally struggled with fever and chills. It was so severe that the priest was called. Last rites were given.

Then, as quickly as he had succumbed to his illness, the young man was well and back to his normal life. This was merely the first of many brushes with death for Wally Pieszka.

CHAPTER 7

THE GERMANS ARRIVE - 1939

The summer of 1939 passed rather quickly. As promised, Wally had gone back for seventh grade and finished his final year of school, the only years of school available at the time in rural Poland. He had spent the summer selling perfume and cologne to the neighborhood women. He dreamed of having his own business someday and being off the farm.

As the summer drew to a close, Wally was accepted in a business school program. The school was many miles away, too far to bicycle, but it could give him the training he needed to become a successful business-man. He would have to spend the week in Bielsko-Biala and come home by train only on the weekends. For Wally, this would be the first time away from home and family. He was excited. But first the task at hand, as with all Polish farmers, was to take out the last of the crop of potatoes. As with all the crops on the Pieszka farm, harvesting would be done by hand. School would not start until October 1.

On August 30, 1939, his mother summoned him. His sister-in-law, Emil's wife Sophia Kadzielnik, had delivered her first baby only two days before. The birth of her daughter took place without a husband. Sophia lived with Wally's family on the farm once Emil was drafted into the Polish army two months before. Emil would not see this child for a very long time.

But Sophia needed medical help. She started bleeding profusely. No one had a car, so Wally was sent with his bicycle to fetch the only med-ical help available, a mid-wife who lived two villages away.

Wally rode to the village and told the mid-wife she was needed in Ilownica at once. He put the woman on the crossbar and began pedaling. She was not light, weighing well over two hundred pounds. He struggled with the pedaling and the steering. All of a sudden, bullets whizzed over their heads. Wally, in a panic, headed for the ditch and crashed into the trees along the roadside. The midwife landed on top of him. Clearly the shots had come from the woods and were intended to either hit them or at least frighten them. While it didn't do the former, it certainly did the latter.

Both lay on the ground waiting for more shots. When none came, the two dusted themselves off and pondered the situation. As no further shots had been fired, they guessed that the shots came from either a fool-ish Pole or one of the dreaded Germans who were said to be amassing in the distant woods. Wally and the midwife arrived at Wally's home within half an hour, and the midwife performed her duties, stemming the bleeding. While this traumatic event ended well, it was the first hint of a German invasion. Wally shared the day's event with his mother and father, but neither of them had any more information about a possible invasion.

The next day, August 31, 1939, an infamous day for Poland, found harvest time in full swing for the southwestern Poles. The potatoes were ripe for harvest in the field. The wheat crop was harvested a month before, ground by the miller in the village, and the ground wheat was safely stored in the Pieszka attic. In spite of nervous talk, harvest was on and the fields were dry.

But that evening brought a new phenomenon to the Polish countryside. From midnight through the rest of the night, the sky was bright with flares. It was like day time, and Wally was immediately awakened from his sleep. Airplanes, clearly not Polish, filled the sky. The roar was continuous and deafening. There were so many planes and they were so big. The family began to expect the worst. Obviously, the Germans were coming. But what could they do about it?

At six that next morning, the Pieszka family arose, did their chores of feeding their animals and ate a traditional farm breakfast. The cereal, bread and butter would suffice as a meal for a while. It would be the last meal before nightfall. Wally's mother brought some bread and water to the field, but that would be it. The crew went to the field.

Harvest was a tiring time, but the now 16-year-old Wally was strong and up to the task. His spade sunk into the ground again and again, prying the potatoes to the surface while his mother gathered them in her apron and carried them to the baskets that were brought to the fields. Wally's father was not very good at digging because of his hand, but he did what he could. The potatoes were piling up and the sweat flowed from all of them.

That night, rumor had it among several of the townspeople that the Germans were still to the south or west. Polish forces were scattered about the area. Unknown to the Pieszkas, the Germans were crossing the border from Czechoslovakia into Poland that day. There was neither radio nor any other communications available to alert the nation of the imminent invasion. Harvest was to continue tomorrow.

Later the next morning, unknown people started to appear in the village. They were escaping the invasion and were leaving their homes, taking a few prized possessions in wheelbarrows and handcarts north to the forests and mountains. One man was wheeling his wife in a wheelbarrow. She appeared crippled or injured. She held a large suitcase in her hands. It was obvious that her husband could not carry the weight of both much longer. Finally, as Wally watched, the woman chose to abandon her suitcase right by the Pieszka home. That suitcase remained with Wally's mother through the war and was returned to the owner in 1945.

The Pieszkas did not fully understand the immediacy of the coming German forces that day, but they could not have fled as this couple was doing. They had animals to mind including a cow, pigs, chickens and even Wally's goat. They had to stay put and finish their harvest.

On September 2, the family again returned to their potato field. In mid-morning, there was an explosion not far away, near the center of the village. They could only guess as to the cause of the sound. Were troops fighting?

Then the Germans appeared. A caravan of large camouflaged tanks, trucks and armed troops with rifles came straight toward the family. The Pieszkas shrank back near the hedge by the border of their property.

The tanks rolled on, straight across the potato fields toward the small Ilownica River. Not a word was spoken among the family. What was there to say? They stood in amazement as their precious potatoes were uprooted by the treads of the tanks. No shots were fired as the menacing horde just kept coming. Everyone was frightened. There was nothing to do. This was their home, and in that ground was the food that stood between them and starvation.

The village of Ilownica was small and the homes were dispersed, as many had a few hectares for their crops and animals. Roads were not surfaced, save some gravel here and there. Through the center of the town ran a small river. It generally flowed within its banks and had only a few feet of water by summer's end. It was deep enough to require a bridge for crossing. That one bridge was the only crossing point for several miles in each direction. While often containing minimal water, at times of the year it flooded, and local boys, including Wally, learned to swim in this narrow stream.

Within a few hours after the appearance of the Germans, word spread that Polish forces had blown up the one bridge over the river in the center of the village. The German tanks came to a halt on the steep southern river bank. Soon, German officers were shouting at the villagers and collecting them into a group near the blown bridge. Wally and his father were included in the roundup.

Many Ilownica residents did not speak German, but it became obvious that the village men were going to be forced to carry the German supplies, ammunition and even the soldiers on their backs across the narrow and shallow river to the north side. To refuse would have been life threatening. All the Germans had loaded rifles and bayonets attached. The water was four feet deep at the blown bridge and only 20 feet wide.

Wally and his father were forced to the water's edge. Even some village women were included in the group, but not Wally's mother or sister-in-law. Wally and his father could not fully understand the orders being given them in German, but they understood that they were being recruited to aid the German forces.

Soon, word spread that a German soldier had been shot. The German officers made it clear that retribution would follow against the villagers. All of the men who had been forced to the river bank were threatened in German with immediate death if the perpetrator did not come forward. The people clearly got the meaning of the German words. With that, a Polish soldier stepped from a building and surrendered, announcing that he was the one who had shot the German. He was not from their village and no one knew him. All were astonished by his courage. A German officer raised his pistol and marched the soldier away. No one heard a shot, but it was quite clear he would not survive the day.

Wally later remembered thinking that if the soldier had been shot in front of the crowd, would that act have further intimidated the crowd or merely made it clear how the next six years would be under the Germans? The soldier had saved wholesale slaughter of villagers, although at that point these rural Poles were totally unaware of the cruelty of which the German forces were capable. Perhaps the German officer was smart in not making the brutality patently obvious that first day. It would come soon enough.

The German soldiers returned to the business of crossing the river. Wally was forced to carry one of the German soldiers on his back across the river. The hobnails of the German's boots dug into Wally's sides and hips. The marks were visible for days. Wally, totally soaked from the water, deposited his soldier on the north bank. The German stayed dry from the knees up.

Wally was not required to carry anything or anyone else that day. By then, the Germans learned that there was a shallower point with less steep banks just a few kilometers to the west. They moved the crossing to this new point. The tanks, trucks and troops could now easily cross.

Some German troops remained in the village that night, but the majority pushed northward toward the Polish opposition. The remaining soldiers chose several houses for their quarters, immediately displacing the owners, who then sought shelter with neighbors and friends.

The next day, searches took place throughout the village. Homes were entered, supposedly looking for Polish troops, but the searches were more destructive than effective. China cabinets with prized possessions were destroyed, even though they were too small to hide anyone. Furniture was ruined. Bayonets were used to spear clothing in the closets, ripping them, in search of these invisible Polish soldiers. This excessive cruelty was clearly done to instill subservience in the Poles.

Soldiers entered Wally's home. A wardrobe was wrecked, as were other household items, but no enemy soldiers were discovered. The German presence was terrifying to these rural people.

The harvest continued with the uprooted potatoes, as well as those still in the ground. The first days of German occupation were over.

The first significant change in the village occurred immediately after September 2, 1939. Signs were placed on some of the houses in the village proclaiming, in German, that the property was that of the Third Reich. Such a sign appeared on the Pieszka home that week. These signs meant that, if requested, the occupants had 24 hours to surrender the residence to the Germans and vacate the premises.

Wally hated that sign with unrelenting passion. Every day that passed was filled with nervous anticipation about whether a request might be forthcoming. Wally became more and more determined to have this sign removed.

Soon, ration cards were issued to the citizens, not to increase the available food, but to monitor what food was available and how it would be disbursed. Food was literally confiscated off shelves and pantries and then carefully parceled out. Stores became empty. Meat, butter and sugar were the most carefully monitored foods.

When Wally's mother first heard of the rationing, she hid some of her chickens in the basement of the house. That way, when the Germans came to demand her eggs, they got less. Even then, the Germans demanded production from the farm animals in outrageous amounts. On one occasion, a German officer tried to tell Wally's mother how many eggs she needed to deliver to the Germans each week. Sophia replied in rather good German that she had learned in her childhood in Silesia, "Don't tell me how many you need, tell the chickens!"

As Wally was to later learn, unlike the larger cities, the rationing in Ilownica was fairly uniform between the Poles and the Jews. In Warsaw, the Jews got a fraction of the food that the other Poles got, and the Poles got less than the Germans.

Other decrees were made throughout Poland. In early October 1939, a curfew was mandated in the larger cities from dusk to dawn. This did not apply to rural farmers and was not enforced outside Warsaw and Krakow. Next, even radios were banned.

There were more decrees aimed only at the Jews. By the end of October there was a census taken of all Polish Jews, and by December, Jewish schools were closed, and praying in synagogues was prohibited.

In Ilownica, all schooling above sixth grade was cancelled, and those surviving classes were now to be taught in German. Teachers fluent in German were hired and the other teachers were terminated. All of Wally's former teachers were soon replaced. Courses now contained German history, language and forced adoration of Adolph Hitler.

In the churches, the priests were to conduct their religious services, not in Polish or Latin, but in German. Often the priests spoke no words aloud, but moved their mouths with their traditional service. There were no longer any sermons.

As summer turned to fall and fall to winter, Polish life in Ilownica changed entirely. Wally knew he had to escape, find a profession and move on, but all this had to be done under the watchful and controlling eyes of German forces. Wally's dreams of business school were dashed. It was not to be. Wally and a friend wracked their brains for something they could do to become more than dirt farmers. They were stuck. With the loss of the business school, he and his friends sat more than a few evenings pondering their future or the lack thereof. He traveled on occasion by foot or bicycle to the two or three nearby villages without success.

In early December, Wally asked about the Urbach family and his friend Regina. When he got no information, his mother finally broke the news to him.

"The entire family just disappeared one night. The Germans closed the store and took over the house. No one knows if the Germans took them, but they are just gone."

No one would ever see the family again. Wally's hatred of the occupation and the Nazis grew even stronger. They took his friend and first love. She was gone.

After the war, Wally learned that the family had been taken to Auschwitz, where they perished.

Wally had a cousin living in a village about twenty miles from Ilownica. Word came that her husband had a shortwave radio and was listening to news from England. Someone in the village got wind of this and the German troops showed up at the house, searched it, and shot the man on his own front steps.

Wally also heard the story of a forced attendance in a town square near Ilownica. The villagers were to cheer the arrival of a German politician. While assembled in the market square, the townspeople were instructed to respond with a "Heil Hitler." As this was happening, one man sneezed. The German troops grabbed the man and sent him to a camp, probably Auschwitz. He never returned.

Life was like that. One day things seemed at least tolerable, and the next day someone you knew or liked was just gone. But there was one constant: the Germans were here to stay with their authority and cruelty.

CHAPTER 8

ANDREW'S ESCAPE

Brother Frank still lived in the neighboring village, but while permitted to continue work as a tool and die maker, his products changed from civilian products to military necessities. He visited less and less as the pressure on his skills became more demanding, but he was safe. The Germans needed Frank. He was married and was living a fairly normal life under the occupation.

Wally's youngest half-brother, Andrew, had become his closest friend. Andrew taught him boy things and helped him with his school lessons. They slept in the same bed for years until the new house was finished and the second bedroom added. Andrew was the quiet one, but he was the one who spent time with Wally and helped him grow up.

In late 1936, when Andrew was 22 years old, he received a notice that he was to take an army physical. Poland, fearing the German growth and the assumption of power by Adolph Hitler, was building an army. The draft was in full force. There was a realistic fear from the Polish leaders that Germany would march east someday and try to reclaim lands that were lost under the Treaty of Versailles, especially Silesia. Andrew went to his physical exam in the bordering town of Bielsko-Biala and passed it with ease. He was a strong, well-developed man by that time.

Andrew was drafted into the Polish army in early 1937 and reported to a Polish army camp. This camp, known by the village name of Oswiecim, became better known when the Germans later changed the camp name to Auschwitz. There he took his military training and remained at the camp for the next year. He was part of the Polish force to withstand a German invasion.

In early 1938, his brother, Emil, also was drafted back into the Polish army. By mid-September 1939, the Polish army was totally routed and Emil was captured, unwounded, and immediately sent to a German POW camp to be held there for the remainder of the war. Andrew was in a different part of Poland, but the crushing defeat was everywhere. The Polish army was collapsing under the blitzkrieg of the German forces.

Andrew's company had begun retreating further east, past Krakow. There were some minor clashes with German troops, but the Poles were moving as fast as they could to stay away from the main bodies of German troops. Soon, the eastern border of Poland with Russia was at their backs. There was no more room to retreat. To most, the only hope of survival was to surrender. Andrew wanted no part of this. He soon realized that to stay with his troops meant immediate capture and confinement, if not execution.

The defense of Poland was a lost cause. Andrew left his rag-tag unit and headed for the forest with a couple of other Polish enlisted men. Andrew's battalion had ceased to exist as the German tanks swept through the mounted Polish cavalry. It was no contest. Most soldiers were taken prisoner. Fortunately, Andrew's departure just a day or two earlier allowed his escape. Unfortunately, he had no clothing other than his Polish uniform.

Andrew wandered the nearby forest for two days. There was no food. The temperature was still mild. Sleeping under the trees was better than in a POW camp, but he was starving. Andrew decided to take a chance and leave the woods for an indirect but safer way home. This route took him into the countryside for a while. He wore part of his Polish uniform although that was an imminent problem. He feared that his clothing would soon lead to his capture by German troops. His goal was to get back to Ilownica and his family. They could hide him until the roundup of Polish soldiers subsided.

Andrew finally stopped at a farm house and pleaded his case to a sympathetic Polish farmer. He was taken into the farmer's house where he got a small but well-cooked meal. Andrew explained his plight to the farmer and his wife. He shared the complete defeat of the Polish army. They suspected that result but had not heard of it for certain.

Andrew was allowed to sleep in the barn that night. In the morning the farmer produced a set of ragged farm work clothes. They fit poorly and had holes, but Andrew had to get out of his uniform. The farmer agreed to burn the Polish uniform, and Andrew set off for home, the only place he knew where he could stay. It took him only two days traveling more directly since he could now walk the roads in relative safety.

Andrew traveled as fast as he could walk without raising suspicion. He made it home and the Pieszka/Kadzielnik family was ecstatic. Andrew was back. His mother was in tears, as the entire village had heard of the defeat of the Polish Army, yet she had no news yet of the safety of Emil or Andrew. She hugged Andrew that evening like a lost child found, as he explained his plight of the last two weeks. He had traveled more than 80 miles on foot.

Andrew took up residence in his old room with Wally. They talked well into that first night, although Andrew was somewhat reserved about his recent adventure. Wally probed, getting only minimal responses. That was Andrew's way. Andrew knew the Germans had come to Ilownica and learned from Wally of the Germans' arrival on the farm and the happenings in the town. Wally talked of his plan of going to a different town to study painting as soon as he could. Andrew explained that he had no plans, as he had no vocation other than working on the family farm. He was envious that Wally at least had a plan.

The peaceful reunion lasted only two weeks. Andrew stayed close to the farm and out of sight. He helped where he could. They were a family again. Perhaps there was someone who may have reported Andrew's presence in the village to the German authorities and mentioned that he had been a Polish soldier. Not all the local people bonded together against the Germans. There were those who sought favor by informing on others, be they Jewish or not. No one would ever learn how the Germans discovered Andrew's presence in the Pieszka home.

It was late one evening when a squad of German troops banged on the Pieszka front door. The family sensed there was trouble. No one called that late in this village with the German presence. Andrew was in the bedroom and knew he had to escape. It was clear that the Germans had come for him. He bolted for the back of the house where there were two windows. He managed to open one and slipped out the small window -- right into the arms of a German soldier! The squad had surrounded the house before the knock on the door.

Andrew was taken by car away from the house to German headquarters for interrogation. For three days, no one knew the fate of this young man. Sophia cried every night, fearing the worst and believing that she was about to lose another son. Emil was missing and now Andrew.

Then, as quickly as he had gone, Andrew was back. Wally was amazed to see Andrew walk into the family home.

Andrew explained his incredible escapade to the family. After those three days of being locked in a room in the German headquarters, a soldier brought him to a large room with a desk and chair. There were several soldiers standing in the room. One was seated at the desk, a German captain who was clearly in charge and took over.

Andrew gaped in surprise because he had known this man when he was at Auschwitz. The man had been a Polish officer. Apparently, the captain agreed to join the German army since then and again was made an officer. The captain also remembered Andrew from Auschwitz. Andrew had been in his company. They had liked each other. There was immediate recognition but no acknowledgment.

The captain barked out, "What are you doing with this man? Don't you know this man was discharged from the Polish army because he has tuberculosis? Get him out of here before we all catch it."

Andrew was immediately shown to the street. No one touched him again. The trip back home was a delight even though it had involved a long walk from from Bielsko. Never expecting such a break, Andrew knew he was one of those lucky people in life who the saints protect. He was home.

Andrew took Emil's place on the farm with the harvest and chores and continued sharing a room with his brother. Wally, now 16, had grown since he had last seen Andrew. They kidded about his size and strength. Life was good but tense.

The Germans were everywhere. Street signs were being changed into German. All Polish customs were gone. Except for Emil, the family was all together.

Andrew continued to live at home for several years and soon had a girlfriend. They were married in 1940 and continued to live in the family home. All would go well for Andrew until late 1941 when the Germans drafted him into their army. He was to follow a very similar path to that of Wally, including training in Germany for infantry duty.

With Andrew being drafted, there were now two daughters-in-law without husbands living with Wally's parents.

CHAPTER 9

APPRENTICE PAINTER

As the months went by, life became more predictable. The Polish people knew how to live under foreign domination. They had survived the Austrians and before that the Russians, Mongols, Ottoman rulers and now the Germans.

But under the Germans, rules were different and much stricter. Only the German language was permitted to be spoken or written. Many of the older locals already spoke some German. The population of Silesia had changed borders and countries often. These residents spoke, although minimally, several languages. For a few years now, their country had been Poland, but the people could never count on who was in charge. As a result, Wally's mother spoke German much better than her sons.

Wally's family had to prove their non-Jewish heritage in order to continue to live in their village. Since there were no county seats or court-houses with documents of birth, marriage or even death records, proof of non-Jewish heritage had to be found elsewhere. Catholic churches kept such records but those records were scattered in many different churches as the people moved, married or found other employment over the generations. The search would need to go back three generations to satisfy the Germans that there were no Jewish ancestors lurking in one's past.

Wally's family began the search. With the help of local priest, Father Niemuk, sufficient records were produced. Wally's family would not be deported for now, and Wally could seek some type of simple employment opportunity.

Since business school was out, and businesses and factories created and run by Polish families now needed a German representative to "manage" them, Wally was out of luck. The former owners stayed on in many cases, but often had little to say in the operation of their old business.

Since Wally had no family business other than farming, and no trade, he needed to find new employment. Under German authority, everyone worked. He and his friend, Edvard Daniel, heard of a possible career in painting. While working as regular house and building painters during the day, they could sign up for two evenings of schooling in the art of commercial painting. If they completed the schooling, they could become painting tradesmen but it would involve an apprenticeship to complete their licensures. While the schooling and the day job of painting were in two different towns, by attending both, they might someday become full-fledged artisans.

The painting apprentice training was located in Skoczow, a village about 25 miles away, while the painting school would be in Bielsko-Biala, the latter being about 18 miles away from Skoczow but farther south. Bielsko itself was about 20 miles from Wally's home. Too far to bicycle every day, Wally and Edvard needed to walk 45 minutes to the Chybie station and then take a train to Skoczow.

Wally and Edvard talked of what they might find in these new towns. Neither had ever been to either place before. Any trips were few and generally consisted of school trips to the forests north of Ilownica. The decision was made. The boys would take the job and enroll in the school. They would have to find boarding in this new town at prices they could afford.

On their first day, both boys walked nervously to Chybie and boarded the train. The train pulled into the Skoczow station 40 minutes later and the boys got off, with simple bags filled with clothing on their shoulders. After a short walk, they found the address they had been given.

When they checked in with the painting company, they quickly learned that they were not the only candidates for painting apprentices. More than 20 young men and boys were gathered for the first day of basic instruction.

The curriculum involved learning better German and giving speeches in German. The evening instructor was Polish, and while friendly, he was required to follow the rules imposed by the new sovereign. No Polish! Only German would be spoken. The new laws caused consternation, and although both Wally and Edvard could mimic, talk with their hands and say some German words, a full conversation was hard. To be instructed in this foreign language would be difficult.

Most of the other apprentices were from nearby Bielsko-Biala and returned home each night after class or after the day's work of painting. By now it was early December of 1939, and the weather was changing. The boys were told, for a price, they could sleep on cots in the painting warehouse in Skoczow. Only Wally and Edvard stayed there. They went home every other weekend, ate as much as they could and then tried to bring some food back to their "room" on Sunday nights. Minimal food was provided with the cots, but the price was steep compared to the wages paid by the company.

The boys earned about 50 marks for the week of painting, and their wages were taxed. One was a German tax and one was actually a tax to fund the rebuilding of Poland! In addition, Wally paid for his room and board in the warehouse. At the end of a week he might be lucky to have 5 or 10 marks left. But the idea was to learn the trade and have his own business. How long Poland was to be ruled by the enemy was not only unknown, but between Wally and his friend, it was not ever seriously discussed. The fate of the Pole was always in someone else's hands.

Both boys wanted to become certified painters, thinking such a position might bring some hope for their future.

The evening classes were about measuring rooms and walls, figuring out quantities of supplies and how the paints were made and mixed. The students learned to estimate the amount of time to complete a painting job so that written bids for a project could be compiled.

In addition, the German lessons began. Wally struggled with the language. He had to learn sounds by rote. They had no books. The instructor would only bring newspapers and booklets for examples of the written word, often documents proclaiming the immortality of Adolph Hitler.

While the business school was run by the kindly Polish man and his wife, it soon became clear that the Polish students were not going to become approved tradesmen. The German students would be the only ones who got certified. This angered Wally but he had no other options. Since all working-age people were required to have jobs, if he couldn't paint, some truly menial task would be assigned to him, so he plugged on in spite of low expectations.

Classes were sometimes monitored by German officers. On one occasion, it was Wally's turn to present material in German to the class. He was to give the life story of the Fatherland, the Reich and Hitler. He spent several days practicing his German lines. As he went to the front of the classroom, his hands started perspiring. He began his presentation. His friend, Edvard, started making silly faces from the back of the room and Wally froze. He couldn't finish his speech. His mind went blank and no German came out. The teacher was disappointed, but the officer was angry. There was an exchange of words in German with the teacher, and the officer left. Wally could barely follow what was said.

Wally soon learned that his actions were to warrant punishment. He was required to copy, by hand, the entire German newspaper that had been brought to class that evening. It had at least a dozen full pages. He went to work on his punishment later that evening. It was impossible. He lost his place, broke his pencil, and then lost what little interest he had. Wally decided to skip around, not doing any section completely, copying only the beginnings and the ends.

The next evening he presented his multiple pages of hand-written text to the German officer along with the newspaper he was to have copied. The officer sat down and pored over Wally's work. This time the sweat started down Wally's back. The officer was reading his work word for word.

"Mr. Pieszka, it would appear you are a cheat. You will spend the weekend thinking about disobeying specific instructions. Report to the military jail at once."

Wally was told the location of the jail. He walked to it. His heart was pounding. Words were spoken at him in rapid German as he was taken to a cell. There was a jug of water, a can for his toilet and a bed. There was no food.

Friday night passed into Saturday. There were no other prisoners and really no guards, but the cell door was locked. Saturday evening came with rumbling in Wally's stomach. There was still no food. He again went to bed hungry. He had not planned to go home that weekend so he didn't worry about what his parents might think. He didn't think Edvard was going home either, so the punishment would not be known to his family.

The next morning, there still was no food, only some more water. About 4 p.m., with a flurry of German words, a guard opened the cell door. Assuming he could leave, Wally hurried out of the cell and the front door. His punishment was over but the realization that the Polish apprentices would never get a certificate as a painting tradesman hurt more than his imprisonment. He could paint with the tradesmen, do the very same job, but not receive the same pay. He would always have to work for someone. Under the occupation, he would never own his own business.

In spite of this disappointment, Wally was learning a trade. It was bearable. It was presumed that the school would take most of two years to complete, but another surprise was in store for Wally.

The owner of the school was drafted into the German army in the summer of 1940. His wife contemplated running the school herself but soon realized that she was not qualified to certify any graduates and did not fully understand the painting business. She decided to close the school. With it went the association with the painting day job.

They were out of work, out of education and out of a place to sleep at the tender age of 17.

Now there was real concern for Wally and Edvard. The Germans required people of Wally and Edvard's age to have a job. Since they had no job, they had to report to the Bielsko employment office which was under German control. Wally went home for a few days and again contemplated his future. He was beginning to lose his childhood confidence that had sustained him thus far. Under the Germans, he had no rights, no control and a bleak future. It seemed so unfair, but the Poles were all helpless. The Jews were even more helpless. He realized that the Jewish merchants in his village were almost all gone, their shops either closed or under the management of some new person, in most case a German and not a Pole. He had no other options. He would report to the employment office.

Edvard and Wally traveled together to the German employment

office in Bielsko. They filled out papers, then sat and waited for an interview. Both listed their short year of painting as their "profession." After a delay, both were ushered into a smaller room with a German officer at his desk. They took the two chairs and sat silently. A rush of German words followed, too fast for Wally to comprehend. When neither moved, the officer said two words that Wally could comprehend. Painting and "Oswiecim."

The boys were handed documents in German. Understanding that they were dismissed, they rose politely and left. As they exited the building, they tried to discover more about their newest employment. With the help of another Pole standing outside the building, they further translated their documents. They had a job. They were laborers assigned to a painting detail as part of a larger workforce that was doing some sort of refurbishing of an old Polish army camp at a place called Oswiecim. Soon, all were calling this place Auschwitz, as the Germans preferred. For right now the larger task was figuring out where it was and how to get there.

Both Wally and Edvard returned home to Ilownica. When Wally explained to his parents what had transpired, they seemed relieved that he would be employed in a field that seemed safe for the moment. Oswiecim was just another place on the Polish map.

Wally decided that he would spend the weekend at home and commence his trip on Monday. He was told that Edvard decided to leave at once. Wally wanted a few more days of comfort before undertaking this unknown mission. He made a promise to himself that he would eat as much as possible before setting out. Wally was now more than 5 feet 9 inches tall and weighed around 150 pounds. He was strong from his boyhood farm work and he had great stamina.

"Moving to another town couldn't be that bad," he said to himself as he went to bed that night.

What could be bad about Oswiecim or Auschwitz, or whatever they called it?

CHAPTER 10

AUSCHWITZ

As Wally spent the last night at home, he was totally unaware of what lay ahead. In twenty-four hours, his visions of a good job would give way to some of the ugliest visions the human mind could ever possibly imagine.

Only years later would even some of the brutal truths of this place come to be known worldwide. This was his immediate future.

Auschwitz was an army barracks formerly used for years by the Polish army. It had been immense, with many buildings and confined areas. Now it was in total disarray. By September 1939, Auschwitz was of no use to the Polish Army, and the Germans quickly came up with a plan for this huge, barren place.

Camps were needed to contain dissidents and troublemakers of the Third Reich. Auschwitz was to become one of these facilities. Jews, gypsies, homosexuals and other "social undesirables" had already been removed from German society and were detained in German facilities. More space was needed for Hitler's "final solution."

Auschwitz would be comprised of several camps as it expanded during the war. There was a forced labor camp. There were detention camps used to restrict certain people from being at large. Often a camp held detainees from a particular country or region. The Germans were orderly in these camps, with complete registration and marked identification of each inmate by tattooing the arms, whether a forced laborer or one scheduled for elimination.

At first, the locals assumed that these prisoners were non-German, anti-fascist or terrorists who would harass the German occupation forces if allowed to roam free. While this was true in part, Auschwitz soon became the killing center of the Third Reich.

Beginning on June 14, 1940, with a few thousand Polish inmates, well over a million people were delivered to these extermination camps. At times, Auschwitz would have more than 100,000 inhabitants at once in its three main camps.

More than a million people who entered the gates of the now electrified barbed wire enclosures of this camp perished. In some post-war reports, it is claimed that as many as four million died at Auschwitz.

In early 1942, while Wally was still working there, the Germans expropriated the entire village of Birkenau, near Auschwitz, in order to increase the size of this particular KZ, the name given to the concentration camps. All the houses there were demolished to build more crematoria.

Next to the last crematorium was the "pyre," a ditch where originally prisoners had been executed by firing squads, burned and then buried before the furnaces were used. When Auschwitz was completed, it was Germany's largest and most efficient exterminating center with its five crematoria and an elaborate railway system to deliver the prisoners there from Hungary, Poland, Romania, Czechoslovakia and Germany itself.

The word outside the camp was that this was to be a manufacturing center that could make anything from a needle to a tank. While there was some manufacturing, the true use of Auschwitz was far from the creation of tanks or needles.

The happenings in the camp were carefully guarded. There were few escapees. Only the ashes of the inmates left the camp.

Those men who moved the bodies from the gas chambers and into the various crematoria were known as Sonderkommandos. They were inmates who were chosen for their strength and they were treated to better conditions including food, clothing and living quarters.

Unfortunately, the downside of being chosen was that every four months these Sonderkommandos were executed and the new group's first job was to dispose of bodies of the men they just replaced. During the course of the use of this KZ, the Germans would go through 14 groups of Sonderkommandos, most groups consisting of 400 to 650 men.

Wally arrived by train at Auschwitz in the late summer of 1940, having been sent by the Arbizund, or employment office.

He walked to the gates that bore the words later to be known around the world: Arbeit Macht Frei -- Work Will Set You Free. Nothing was further from the truth. The only ways to leave were either by shipment to another work camp or by death.

Wally had no idea what he was about to see.

At the time he started to paint at Auschwitz, village people knew nothing specific about the camp. To Wally, his assignment to paint at Auschwitz was both good and bad. It was a job, and that was good in these times. It was bad because it was far from home, requiring him to sleep in a barracks outside the main camp itself during the week. He could return home only for an occasional weekend. For boarding and for his food, Wally was required to pay dearly from his meager earnings. There weren't a lot of other opportunities coming available for a barely-educated young Pole.

Upon entering the camp, a German soldier commanded Wally to read a sign. It told him that he was not to watch what went on here. The soldier informed him that he must sign a book. Wally had no idea what his signing meant, but he signed his name. He was informed that he would have to sign again every time he entered or left the camp. His first signing on going inside the camp said that he would not see anything. The second time, on leaving the compound for his barracks, he again signed verifying that he had seen nothing while there.

His very first signing was about the only time it was the truth. At that point, he had seen nothing.

Wally first was taken to a barracks, number 20-25. He saw no one that he recognized. Although he looked for his friend who had also been assigned to Auschwitz, he would not see Edvard ever again. Much later, he learned that young Edvard died of tuberculosis during the occupation of Poland.

His barracks was a simple building with bunk beds stacked three high. As luck would have it, the young Pole was assigned the top bunk. For heat, there was a small stove in one corner and a supply of wood outside. It was up to the occupants to bring the wood in and keep the fire going during the night. Some nights the watcher would fall asleep and the fire would go out. The men awoke freezing. Each man was given two blankets and a straw-filled pillow upon arrival. Without the heat of the stove, they were soon bone-chillingly cold. Wally once was the man who fell asleep, and he heard about it.

The other men in Wally's barracks were almost all Polish and ranged in age from his tender 17 to men in their late 40s. They were forbidden to speak anything but German, but once the doors closed for the evening, Polish was often spoken.

While these men came to know each other, there was a fear of becoming close, as people seemed to disappear so often. It was better not to make friends. This mental separation of men brought together in work, training or a war itself would be so utterly different from most fighting forces that were mixed together into combat units. Wally would make no friends. There was no comradery.

A dining hall was located near their barracks. The painters shared the eating space with groups of laborers in the various other specialties including plumbing, electrical and other basic construction jobs. The food consisted of cabbage, potatoes and some vegetables, but never meat. Meat was reserved for the German soldiers.

Wally, in his usual behavior of always pushing the envelope, learned that he could enter the German mess, not speak, and get the higher class of food, including meat. He would successfully do this the rest of his time at Auschwitz.

Each group wore a different color set of clothing. Painters had three sets of white, but soon they were covered with the colors that they had been applying. The other trades wore different colored uniforms. Other than the occasion of eating together, there was little mixing of the various trades.

The barracks were in a separate area of the KZ, away from the facilities containing the maximum confinement populations known as Auschwitz I or Birkenau, sometimes called Auschwitz II. The new extermination camp at Birkenau, being quite far away, was unseen by Wally's group of painters, as there was no reason to paint these areas of death.

Wally's group painted offices that had been created within larger spaces. On one occasion, some were to paint in a large house that sat just outside of the barb wire. It had a view of a substantial portion of the camp. Wally knew that this was the home of the head of the camp, Herman Hoss. Hoss in 1946, after being convicted of war crimes against humanity, was hanged in the camp from an area that was in full view of his former house.

During that first week, Wally was terrified of the things he saw and some of the noises that he heard. He was more afraid of the Germans and what they might do to him if he violated one of their rules or made some other mistake. This fear started on the very first day for this teenager and would never leave while he painted there.

On the third night in the new barracks, Wally dreamed. The dream soon changed to a nightmare that men were chasing him and trying to beat him. With his thrashing, he fell from the top bunk onto the wooden floor. Fortunately, he was only bruised. While nothing was broken, he was still sore for a few days. After that night, Wally made sure the outside of his blanket was tucked in tightly each night as he fell asleep.

As the second week passed, talk of payday was a chief conversation point. They received pay every two weeks, then the men were allowed to go home for a weekend. For Wally, this required a two kilometer walk and two train trips just to get to Chybie. Before the weekend release, three things happened. First, the men received a payment for their work. Second, money for the room and board they received was subtracted from their pay. Third, the two taxes were taken out. Then he signed the book swearing that he had seen nothing while he was in the camp. In the end, the worker walked away with just a few marks in his pocket for his two weeks of labor.

Wally's crew also painted various signs in the camp, among other projects. On one occasion, Wally and his troop painted what appeared to be a large common shower area. Only years later was Wally to learn the true use of that room.

One week, Wally helped paint two buildings with a concrete wall ten feet high at the north end of the space between them. Even in 1941, Wally could see bullet markings on the concrete wall. He was told by another painter that some of the inmates were shot against that wall before the workers had arrived on site.

41

Wally returned home that second weekend where he ate heartily and slept in a bed that was not plush but a lot better than his third tier bunk. Sunday night came quickly and he took extra food from his parents' home for the trip back. Upon his arrival, he again signed the book that he would watch nothing and see nothing. Painting was boring but time consuming.

There just wasn't much else to do. Wally was moved from building to building as needed for the painting. The places he painted were often offices for German officers and personnel. After a while, he was permitted to walk to these various assignments as he became familiar with the layout of the camp. This first camp outside the fences principally held the laborers and many of the German military assigned to Auschwitz.

Train tracks, however, came right up to Camp 1, and here Wally started seeing those things he had signed papers to swear he hadn't seen. So far the laborers in barracks 20-25 had not seen the death of any inhabitants of the detention camps. This was about to change.

Often when trains arrived, Wally could observe people of all ages being instructed to exit the train cars. The cars were more like those used to haul cattle or other livestock. Upon their exiting, Wally could see that the people were being divided into groups. He could tell that the strong males always seemed to be in one group, while women and children made up several different groupings. He did not know why.

Later, he learned that the first group consisted of those men capable of hard labor, or sometimes, skilled labor for the German war machine. Another group was women capable of working specific jobs. Groups of children too small to work often made up a separate group. Wally just watched and moved on.

Wally's supervisor was an Austrian. He expected competent and rigorous work, but was ultimately fair with the crew. He permitted the 20 or so men to take a few breaks and speak their native tongue when no German soldiers were around. Most of the men were too scared to talk much, especially about any of the happenings of the camp they might have seen.

On one occasion that first year, a prisoner asked Wally for bread. Wally shared a piece of bread with him. Within a few days, the prisoner asked Wally for money or he would tell the authorities that Wally had been supplying food to the prisoners. Wally knew it was a crime to give anything to a prisoner. He was terrified. Here was the very thing he had been warned of. Would this be fraternizing with prisoners? This was clearly forbidden. But was merely giving a crust of bread to a hungry man such an act?

Wally felt trapped. He chose after much thought to mention the instance to his supervisor. Wally waited for a reprimand, but it didn't come. It seems the supervisor took the initiative and informed his German military counterpart that this prisoner had been harassing his men for food.

The prisoner just disappeared. Wally hoped that he was just moved to another part of the camp. As he was there longer, he was learning that this probably wasn't the man's fate.

After several months on the Auschwitz I premises, Wally was walking to a project when he noticed a train arriving. As he walked, the train came to a stop and the doors of the cars were unlocked by German troops. SS officers stood in the rear. Wally later heard that the train came from Romania.

The doors stood open, but no one exited the cars. There were shouts from the German troops, which Wally assumed to be orders to come out, but no one came.

Finally, troops entered the cars and began throwing naked bodies of men, women and children from the train onto the ground. Wally had no idea if death had come from starvation, the lack of air or just exposure. The corpses built up around the doors of the rail cars. The officers were huddled in a conference, and then orders were shouted to the troops. Soon, trucks arrived and the bodies were unceremoniously tossed into their beds and driven off toward the forest to the northwest of the camp.

Wally went back to work. While it was not unusual to see these prisoners arrive naked, he couldn't understand why every one of them had died on that train. But it wasn't his problem. He had seen more than he could comprehend already.

That evening, fires were visible in the forest, and the smell of burning flesh permeated the air. There was no doubt in Wally's mind as to the source of the flames and the stench.

Life at Auschwitz had reached a different level. There were now too many sights that he did not "see," according to the log book, and there would be even more of these each day, each week and each month that followed.

Later that month, Wally saw a conveyor in Camp 2 coming from a building. He had never been in or near that building and security was even tighter for that area. Wally was painting what he believed to be a hospital or medical office. At first he was confused by the presence of the conveyor. On his third or fourth day in that location, the purpose of the conveyor became painfully obvious, as he saw it filled with bodies of naked men and women being transported from one building to another.

He closed his eyes. Yet another thing he "hadn't seen." There were more and more incredible acts of misery, suffering and death being witnessed by Wally and his fellow workers. But what could they do? They were nobodies struggling to survive. Memories of these awful things had to be pushed to the back of one's mind or one could go insane.

Wally continued in this job for more than a year, painting while separately trying to unsee what he was seeing. His visits home were his salvation. He knew the war was raging based on idle chatter he overheard from the soldiers at Auschwitz. The word at home was that the Germans were pushing toward Russia. It was claimed that Stalin broke his treaty with Hitler. The Soviets had stood by while Germany invaded Poland, even though Great Britain had declared war on Germany on September 3.

On September 17, however, the Soviets moved into eastern Poland to occupy their "sphere of influence."

Until Germany made a surprise attack on the Soviet Union in June of 1941, Hitler had kept the war on only one front. The war was now expanding.

CHAPTER 11

THE PHYSICAL

May 13, 1942, was a day like all the rest. The earth was warming, but the routine did not change. Up at 6 a.m. with a quick wash of the face. Pull on the same paint-stained shirt and pants as yesterday. Quickly eat a very average breakfast and head out the doors of the barracks to learn where one would paint today.

Yesterday had been a bit unusual. The crew was taken to a large room with what appeared to be water spigots high on the wall. It was different from the showers they had painted a few months before. The construction was old but clearly recently rebuilt. Larger double doors gave access to the room.

While part of the crew had started painting the walls already, it was Wally's first trip to this building. No one spoke of anything. Wally wondered the purpose of such a large room with overhead water. He was not to be at Auschwitz long enough to find out its purpose.

A German officer came up to Wally as he was about to open the paint. With brush in hand, he quickly rose as the officer approached him. Not to do so could result in some form of discipline.

While Wally could see the name of the officer on his blouse, he couldn't pronounce it, so he remained quiet. The officer tried to call Wally by his last name and mispronounced it. He clearly had Wally's attention.

The German's words flew fast. Wally only understood some of the words, and finally got the gist after a few moments. He had to go home as quickly as possible. He was being excused from further work that day. It had to be his family! Who had died? Who was injured? Why should he be sent home? Was this truly an emergency? His head was spinning.

Wally sprinted to his barracks. A fast change of clothes and he was off for the train station at a trot. The wait for the second train seemed forever. Finally the train for Chybie pulled in. There were few people aboard as it was now afternoon. He took a seat and just stared at the seat in front of him. His mind came up with a dozen scenarios, all of them frightening.

The train finally stopped. Wally tore out the door and began the 45-minute walk to his home town. It was shorter if he cut through the woods rather than go by the roads. It also helped that it was mostly straight downhill. He ran as quickly as he could. It was late afternoon by the time he arrived. Wally rushed in and saw his mother, father and sister-in-law. A wave of relief came over him.

After a quick kiss from his mother, she reached over to the table and retrieved a letter. She handed it to Wally. It was in very formal printing and all in German. Between Sophia and Wally, they were able to decipher the principal concept of the letter. Wally was to take a physical to see if he was fit for German military service.

His father learned of the letter's contents as Wally and Sophia discussed the meanings of certain words. Shock was all over his father's face. While Wally was his only biological child, his three step-sons were already being deprived of their liberty by the Germans, whether by forcing Frank to work for them, interning Emil as a POW of the Germans, or allowing Andrew's narrow escape from the German draft with the "tuberculosis" maneuver. Now Wally was in danger, too.

"They run over my country, close my painting school, send me to work in a place unfit for humans, and now they want me to go fight for them. I will not go!" Wally yelled at his parents.

Only days away from his 19th birthday, anger finally flashed in this youth. His mother and father spent time talking of the various options available to their son. Other village men had been conscripted. Most were able to write their families after being drafted, while some just seemed to disappear. A solemn evening meal followed with more talk but no viable decision was reached. Wally went to his bed in despair. He decided he had to see his parish priest.

The next morning, Wally awoke early. He wanted to tell his priest all his frustrations. The priest was thought to be one of the wisest men in the surrounding villages. Wally walked six miles to the neighboring village of Rudzika. Father Stanislov Niemuk invited Wally into the rectory and asked how he could help. Father Niemuk was the one who taught two hours of religion each week in Wally's grade school.

"The Germans want to draft me, Father. I am to take a physical tomorrow in Strumien," Wally blurted out.

He also told the priest of the sign on the family door proclaiming the home to be German property. He talked of his father losing his railroad pension when the Germans took over. He explained his disgust with the German occupation in short bursts of Polish. His manner of expressing his feelings was not lost on Father Niemuk. He then shared a few of the things he had seen at Auschwitz.

The priest took Wally's hand and led him to the church next door to the rectory. There were no services going on. They entered together and approached the altar.

"Wally, what will you do? Where will you go? What will you eat?"

Wally mentioned going to the mountains as he had heard others had done. "They may kill your family if you don't show up for the conscription physical," the priest responded. Wally knew he had no real plan.

The man and the almost man sat in silence for a few minutes, each contemplating his next statement. The priest spoke first.

"You must go. Then go with God, my son. He will protect you." The priest concluded these words with a blessing, as he placed his hand on Wally's head. As Wally left the church, the priest reminded him, "Do not tell anyone that you have been with me and that we spoke in Polish."

In the morning, his decision finally was reached, Wally left for the physical as directed. He had not mentally committed to anything more than submitting to the exam. Perhaps he would fail the physical and all the worry was for naught. As he thought more, he realized that he was in fine physical shape. He knew in his heart that he would be found fit.

The physical was to be done at a German facility at Strumien, the very town where he had painted almost two years ago. He was required to be there at 8 a.m. the following day. The best way to get there was by bicycle, rather than walking and taking a train, even though the trip was almost 18 miles. The rest of the day passed slowly with depressing thoughts. Supper with his parents was a somber occasion.

Wally was up the next day at 5 a.m. He ate a quick breakfast and started the trip. He arrived well before 8 a.m. By the appointed time there were 40 to 50 men in the building, mostly young. The majority were Polish.

Wally spoke to no one. He was taken into a room by himself. The doctor was tall, thin and wore a grey cover-up, not a uniform. Wally tried to follow the instructions, so it took some time for him to completely comprehend. The doctor tested Wally's eyes and hearing, listened to his heart and had him flex in various positions. His reflexes were checked and the doctor left the room. Almost immediately, an officer informed him that he had passed. In his best German, Wally responded, "I will not go! You took our house. You stopped my father's pension. I will not go."

The officer, who Wally later learned to have been a Polish army officer before getting a German commission, looked at him with a sad face. He knew this reaction and knew it would be fatal in the end.

"Take a seat out front and wait for me. I will be a while," said the officer. Wally took a seat by himself and waited.

The wait was long as other men came and went through the physical process, but none were directed to sit where Wally was. He had nothing to do but contemplate his future. The picture was not happy one. Either way, he was in for some very hard times.

The officer reappeared about 3 p.m. and asked Wally why he was refusing to go. There were some Polish words mixed in with the German, and this surprised Wally.

"I don't want to go. The Germans have put a sign on my parents' house that it is the property of the Deutsche Reich. That means they can take it any time they want. Why would I want to fight for a country that takes its soldier's home?"

The officer pondered the outburst for a moment and said. "How did you get here?" Wally responded by his bicycle. The officer then said, "Get your bicycle and follow me."

Wally went outside and grabbed his bicycle. The officer opened the trunk of a military-looking car, took the bicycle and put it in the trunk. "Get in. Now tell me how to get to your house." Wally got in the passenger side and directed the officer where to head.

Within half an hour they arrived in front of Wally's home. The officer instructed Wally to take out his bicycle and find a hammer. Wally's father quickly found a hammer and returned to the front of the house. Both stood in absolute amazement as the officer walked to the front of the house, pried off the wooden sign with the infamous declaration of German ownership, and handed the hammer back to Wally.

"Now await further instructions. You will get a date to report for duty." With that the officer tossed the sign into the car and drove off.

Wally informed his mother of what had happened. Nothing would ever come of the removal of the hated sign. While terrible things would happen to this house over the next three years, no German ever tried to confiscate it. It seems that Wally's forcefulness and logic had brought a positive result.

Wally went to bed that night with dreams of his youth and nightmares of his future. In spite of the suffering and death he had seen visited on the inmates of that terrible place at Auschwitz, he had been fed, housed and paid. However, if Germany could treat the people he had seen at Auschwitz in such a manner, would Germany treat its conscripted soldiers any better?

The next day, May 16, Wally returned to Auschwitz, where things had changed. He was shown to a new barracks with a different company. The food was better and the beds were not three high. This new comfort was to be short lived. Apparently the camp was aware that he would soon be drafted and was just awaiting orders. He was no longer a poor Pole working for his bread. He was assigned no work!

Wally was worried, as any potential draftee would, that he was soon to be called up. This was not the usual concern of a volunteer or a young man called up to proudly serve his own country. This was forced labor to enter another man's army and to fight an enemy who was not his enemy, and perhaps even die for a cause that was not his cause. Wally kept thinking over and over that the Germans had no right to do this, but he kept his anger hidden.

On the third day of waiting, a voice from behind him yelled out, "Pieszka, you must return home immediately."

The German officer standing behind him signaled that he should leave the job right then. There could only be one reason. He had been drafted.

Wally returned to the barracks, changed from his painting uniform and caught the two trains home. It would again take him only part way and he would walk. The two rides seemed to take forever. He walked and ran through the woods to his home from the Chybie train station.

When he walked in the front door, he was relieved. There were his father, mother, sister-in-law and his new baby niece. They just looked at him sadly.

He knew what was next. He was to become a German soldier. There were no options remaining.

CHAPTER 12

TRAINING IN GERMANY

His mother spoke first. "You have been called up. You must report tomorrow for military service."

In spite of knowing it would happen sometime, Wally's knees shook and fear spread throughout his body. His hands trembled. It was May 19, 1942. In four more days, he would turn 19, and he was being forced into the German army.

The evening was to be his last with the family for a long time, perhaps really the last of all. Supper was cooked, and Mother spared no food in her preparation. She knew bad days were ahead for Wally.

In spite of the favorite dishes sitting in front of him, Wally had no appetite. He ate little and he went to bed as soon as he could. But sleep wouldn't come. Hostile, scary dreams flashed through his head. What was going to happen?

Wally arose early. His mother was already up cooking. He was to report to the train station at Chybie, take it to Bielsko and be there by 10. The walk was the same one he took the day before from Chybie, in the other direction. His father accompanied him, but they talked little.

Arriving in Bielsko well before 10, Wally and his father sat and waited. There were dozens of other young men at the station, as well as a couple of German enlisted men. There was no train yet. Time moved slowly for Wally.

About 11:30, one of the German soldiers announced in German that there was a problem with the train. It would not be coming today. The recruits were to go home and return tomorrow at the same time.

Wally and his father again took a train to Chybie and then walked from the train station to their home. As before, there was little conversation. The impending feeling of doom remained, with only a single day of respite.

On arriving home, they informed his mother of the delay and sat down to an early supper. Not expecting her son home, it was a simpler meal, but Wally still had no appetite. The family talked after dinner. There was some discussion of where Wally might be going. Could he write the family from his new location? Was it in Poland or somewhere else? How long would this training take? No one knew, as no information had been forthcoming from anyone in charge other than where and when to report.

The next day, Wally and his father repeated the process. A walk to Chybie and a train to Bielsko. But this time there was a change of trains in Rudzica, and they missed it. Wally and his father both were nervous about the delay, but a second train arrived. They boarded it for Bielsko and hoped for the best.

When they got to Bielsko, the troop train was already loaded and the men counted. Wally hurried aboard after only a quick hug and words of goodbye from his father. Wally was on his way to someplace for some military training. His head spun. No one in the train was talking. Fear was in the eyes of every single recruit.

There were no stops and no train changes, and the train rolled on for hours. Finally, Wally made out a few German words. They were going to Saarbrucken, Germany. Wally had no idea where that was. He learned that he was to join the Ninth Lancer Regiment, an infantry division. There was a young recruit in the seat next to him, but he dared not speak to him. Who was he? Polish or German? Wally sat quietly. He did hear a few others quietly speaking Polish. The train rolled on.

The men slept in their seats and arrived in Saarbrucken early the next morning. They had a meal only last evening, but no breakfast. His stomach growled. Through the night, Wally recognized a few of the city names on the station boards, including Breslow and Berlin. The three cars of recruits went on with a minimum of stops.

Arriving at yet another station, Wally was able to read the city name of Saarbrucken. It was the last stop. Men began exiting the train. The recruits were marched to the camp from the railroad station. They weren't very organized. The sergeant in charge kept yelling things, but Wally had no idea what he was saying. They were marched to a mess hall and fed breakfast. The time allotted was minimal. The men gulped down their meal and were off again as a group.

Next they entered a large building with racks of clothing and material. Several German soldiers stood behind. These soldiers would eye each individual and start tossing items of clothing at them. Perhaps they were judging each man's size. No one was asked his size, but then Wally never knew his size anyway, as all his clothes were either hand-me-downs or sewn by his mother.

Wally collected three pairs of underwear and socks, but only two pairs of pants and two shirts. He was given two jackets, neither of which was heavy weight. He was tossed a pair of boots, a German cap, a backpack, pillow and a blanket. The men were then told to remove their civilian clothes, wrap them in a bundle and place their name on the bundle. They were told these would be shipped home. They were then shown their barracks and allowed to use the toilets before being formed up again for a special presentation. An officer addressed the group, now including many other men who obviously arrived by other trains from various other towns and villages. There were now several hundred men on the parade ground.

The officer spoke in crisp German, of which Wally could understand only a part. He recognized words like Hitler, army, fighting and brave. He caught that the gist of the officer's speech, that it was historic to give one's life for his country. But Wally's country was Poland, not Germany. Why would he ever want to give up his life for Germany?

After an hour of standing at attention, the group was dismissed into smaller units. Wally's group consisted of about three dozen men. An evening meal was served in the mess hall and the men were marched as a unit to that meal.

Later, they had a bit of free time in the barracks. It was clear that the men were a mixture of Poles and Germans. Wally recognized a man from the train in Bielsko, but there was no one from Ilownica. A few of the men chatted, but soon each man fell into his bunk. Wally was once again in a top bunk.

The next day started before dawn to the sound of someone yelling that they should "fall out" and assemble. The men rushed to pull on their new uniforms and go outside. There was no breakfast, yet they were to start a strengthening program with a myriad of calisthenics. There were pushups and leg lifts, arm rolls and toe touching. Then the routine was repeated. Within minutes, Wally's body ached. He struggled to keep his arms aloft in the twirls. His abdomen ached from the leg lifts.

Finally, they were marched to the mess hall for breakfast. Again, the meal was rushed, food gobbled, and a quick return to training. The men were marched to a different building and received a rifle and some ammunition. One of the more experienced men noticed that instead of metal or copper, the bullets appeared to be made out of wood, but shaped just like metal bullets. Perhaps it was cheaper or safer, but Wally had no idea.

What followed next was instruction of how to disassemble a rifle, clean it, lubricate the parts and reassemble it. He had seen guns before, but he had never touched one. They did this drill over and over. Then there was a demonstration of how to load the bullets into the weapon. Wally had no idea how to do this, either.

The afternoon was filled with the drill of loading and unloading a rifle. Then there was another presentation about Hitler and his life. Over the two weeks of training, Wally was indoctrinated with every aspect of the life of Adolph Hitler that the army wanted him to know.

The next day there were more calisthenics and drills. But on the third day, the men were instructed to form up and bring their rifles. The group of 20 or so men was taken to a range with targets. They were instructed on safety and when to shoot. A half-dozen men at a time approached a wooden barrier and were given instruction on firing at a target a few dozen meters in front of them. They were told how to aim and pull the trigger. Soon, it was Wally's turn. Having never shot a gun before, he held it loosely against his shoulder. Perhaps some of the German explanation that he didn't comprehend had warned him to press the stock of the rifle firmly against his shoulder, but Wally missed that part.

Wally then pulled his first trigger. The rifle slammed into his shoulder and almost knocked him down. At first the instructor merely chuckled, but then he yelled words at Wally that went by without any understanding. Nevertheless, Wally got the message. Keep the stock tight to the shoulder.

He fired again and the recoil was not nearly so bad. Wally continued to fire, and then stepped back as others took his place, only to return again to the barrier. Wally never hit the target. The instructor yelled more words at him that he couldn't understand. What Wally did learn was if you shot poorly, you had to do more pushups right there. Wally did pushups continuously until his aim improved. After a few days, he became more proficient with his rifle, and the pushups subsided.

The men spent the next few days working with their rifles. Then they were introduced to machine guns, the use of bayonets and the firing of pistols. Meanwhile, they received more blankets and equipment.

One day they were instructed on how to pull a pin on a hand grenade and toss the grenade after counting to three. None of the grenades were real, but the routine was followed again and again. Each day the men received more physical training, more political indoctrination and more shooting practice. As the days passed, the men were becoming more physically fit.

The men were forced to swear a loyalty oath to faithfully support Adolph Hitler and the Third Reich. Wally did not so swear, but merely moved his mouth. He felt neither allegiance nor loyalty, only conscription. This was followed by a toast to the Fuhrer. They were given a liquid in a real glass for the toast. The drink was sour and probably some sort of wine. Wally swallowed it and spoke no words.

To Wally's great surprise, they were required to write home every day. They could write in their native language and were to tell their families how well they were treated and how they were serving the Fuhrer. He did receive a few letters from his mother which were sad and teary. She did acknowledge that she received his clothing package in good condition.

On the fifth day, the men were informed that each would be photographed alone in his new uniform. Wally posed for the photographer with a stern and somber face. The next day, his photograph confronted Wally from the backside of a postcard that had been given to him that morning. He was to fill out the front with a message of positive words and address it to his parents. He did so and turned the card into his training corporal.

As the end of the second week neared, rumors began to circulate.

53

They were going to Italy, or Yugoslavia, or, scariest of all -- the Russian Front. That night, Wally had another nightmare and fell out of his top bunk onto the floor, bruising his arm, but suffering no further injury. His mind would not quit worrying about where he might be headed next.

On the final day, the men were sent to a building where they received a comb, toothpaste, a toothbrush and a safety razor, but no lather, just a bar of soap. Wally rarely had to shave, so this wasn't a real problem. The men also received a cup, a plate and various utensils.

Now armed with a rifle, a pistol, a bayonet and no ammunition, the 14-day warrior was about to be sent into battle, somewhere.

The last day was filled with speeches on the parade ground. The speeches concerned how to be faithful to Hitler, and reiterated the story of the life of Adolph Hitler. Wally could never forget Hitler's birthday, April 20, 1888.

In those 14 days, Wally had not seen a woman or a child and had never been allowed off the base, but he now knew a lot more about calisthenics and Adolph Hitler.

The final equipping had been done, and they boarded another train. The men were now convinced that they were headed east, which likely meant Russia. This was somewhat confirmed when each man was issued a woolen half-coat, although they received no gloves.

The next part of this young man's forced adventure was about to commence.

CHAPTER 13

RIDE TO THE RUSSIAN FRONT

The two weeks of training were over. Wally had a gun at his side for the first time in his life outside the camp.

As the training went on, he had been given little live ammunition. The early training was done only with blanks. When finally given real ammunition, Wally had been pathetic. How did the Germans expect a rural Polish man to become proficient with a rifle in less than a week with live ammunition? He wondered if his becoming a good marksman made any difference to the Germans who were training him. Perhaps he was nothing more than another silhouette for the enemy to train its weapons on. It seemed that he wasn't being prepared for anything except to die for the "Fatherland." At least now he could hit wooden targets. What would he do when the target was a human being?

It was now official. The newest recruits were being sent "east." It didn't take much of a brain to figure out that the Germans meant Russia.

The truce between Hitler and Stalin had been broken months before. It was well known that Hitler was moving his armies toward important Russian city-centers. Probably Leningrad and Stalingrad, perhaps even Moscow itself. Some men talked among themselves about their ultimate destination, but few knew geography and fewer still knew where these cities were located.

Wally and his unit were loaded on a train car, similar to a cattle car. There were no bunks. Fortunately, it was early summer and warm. The train cars had a smell Wally could not recognize from his farm experience. Wally thought it might be the smell of confined people being transported by the Nazis. There were no provisions for food or relieving oneself in the rail cars. There was a cooking car attached to the train and every so often the train would stop, pull onto a siding, and allow the soldiers to get off for a while, relieve themselves and be fed. The food was good and plentiful.

During these stops, the men often received further training in the carbine and small arms. For the first time, there was training with machine guns. All the ammunition was now live. Wally was assigned to fire one of these massive machine guns. Two soldiers per gun, one firing and the other feeding the cartridges into the slot. It was obvious that this minimal training was more to scare advancing troops than to kill them.

The soldiers, almost all of whom were Polish, realized they were traveling through Poland. Wally recognized the route since his father had often spoken of his travels as a conductor.

The train stopped in Chybie, only a few miles from Wally's home. There to Wally's surprise was an old friend of his father, Mr. Cebula. They talked briefly and Wally found out that his father had been waiting for his train and had food for him, but they missed each other. Mr. Cebula promised to tell Wally's father that they met. Soon, the train departed. Wally's heart was broken. He so missed his family and to have come so close to seeing his father saddened him even more. He hated the draft, the German army and just about everything.

Within a couple of hours, the train pulled into Krakow. The troops were told that they would be here for two days. They were moved to what were called transit train cars for housing. These train cars were often used in the field as quarters. They had bedding of sorts on straw pallets. Wally had his bedroll and was adequately comfortable. It was certainly an improvement over the floor of the train car.

An hour or so after the move, another soldier told Wally that someone was looking for him. He left the quarters and walked toward the train station. There, coming toward him, was his father.

"How did you catch up to us, Papa?" he asked.

"I took the next train after you left," his father responded. "Mr. Cebula told me that you had stopped in Chybie. I just missed you, so I took a chance and followed you. They told me that your train was headed for Krakow and might stop."

They hugged and held each other. Wally was amazed that his father found him, considering the limited methods of communication that existed in Poland.

"Where are you going, son?" Papa asked.

"We don't know for sure, but some think Russia. What else is to the East?" Wally responded.

His father just shook his head. That could only be war with the Russian troops. They were brutal and Wally's father had heard all the tales of the Russians. His heart sank.

"I have brought you some food. Your mother sends her love," Papa said. With that he opened his knapsack and pulled out freshly baked bread, jams and pickles. Wally took it greedily. How could he know what lay ahead? So far, the food was adequate, but who knew for how long? Wally stuffed it all in his duffle among his clothes.

The time passed quickly. They had been speaking in Polish. They were careful to stay away from all the others. The commander had excused Wally from the morning exercises, one of the few gracious acts Wally ever received from a superior officer. It was early June and the sky was blue. The sun was warm.

With tears in their eyes, Wally and Papa parted. Neither knew when, if ever, their next meeting might take place.

Two days later, the soldiers were switched back to the cattle cars and the engine lurched forward into the unknown. Each day the train traveled only a few dozen miles. Often it took a side rail as another train passed by, some with heavy military equipment on flatbeds. At each stop, the men exercised and practiced their soldiering. Wally's aim had improved. He also learned to hold the rifle butt even tighter against his shoulder with live ammunition.

There were field tactics taught as well. The men practiced taking a house as if they were under fire, with the occupants defending the house firing blanks. Wally only attacked the house, he never defended it. Perhaps there was a message here that the Germans did not envision Wally being the attacked. He certainly wasn't aggressive and this may have shown. Then again, the Germans may have only had plans to attack, not defend. Their mantra was only to attack. Let the enemy defend.

The days passed slowly. It was almost a month before they pulled into a large city, Kiev. One could tell that the city had been strenuously defended without success. It was in ruins, but clearing the rubble in the city was now in the hands of the Germans.

The next day their train moved out. In a matter of three hours it again came to a halt. The men jumped out and began relieving themselves. As Wally watched, he could see peasants walking parallel with the track on a dirt side road. They shuffled lifelessly.

One woman was walking alone with a tiny baby in her arms. She appeared to be chewing something. After chewing for a few moments, she pried open the baby's mouth and spit the contents of her mouth into the baby's mouth. She then took another handful of seeds and put them in her mouth and started chewing again. They looked like sunflower seeds. She did the same things after chewing a few more moments.

Apparently, the woman had nothing to give her baby to eat but these tough seeds. Wally took the remaining hunk of the bread his mother baked for him and approached the woman. She was painfully thin and short. Her hair was covered by a babushka, her body shapeless and her face gaunt.

The woman stopped and stared at Wally. She neither tried to walk away nor approach. It was clearly an act of indifference. Whether it was a look of contempt or one of fear, Wally could not tell. Wally handed the piece of bread to the woman. She eyed the morsel for a few seconds and reached for it. Her hand touched Wally's and he could feel her callouses and rough skin. This woman had not had an easy life. The woman drew the bread back toward her chest, nodded imperceptibly and walked on.

As Wally turned to go back toward the train, he saw his sergeant coming toward him, the German words flying. He caught some of the tirade, the gist of which was that she was Russian, she was the enemy. How did he dare to share the German army food with the enemy? Wally wanted to explain that the morsel was not German food, but Polish, however, his lack of command of German would have made it futile. He accepted his punishment, more exercise.

The next day, the train ground to a halt. Wally's unit unloaded and the troops were instructed to carry all of their gear, as the train ride portion of their voyage was over. Now they would walk. With all of his property in a bag slung over his shoulder, or in his pockets, Wally started walking.

They were in the middle of nowhere, going somewhere or perhaps to nowhere. By now, Wally had befriended one Polish man, Josef Korzeniowski, from Rudzica. They spent time talking as they walked mile after mile.

Over the next few days, the German unit found enemy forces for the first time. The Russian opposition was offering limited resistance. They were hiding in the trees, on top of hills and low mountains, behind barns and in ditches. The Germans returned fire often and even made a few sorties toward this hidden enemy. In most cases, Wally's troops hunkered down until the danger passed.

On this occasion, Wally was almost seriously wounded when a bullet careened off his helmet. Other than a headache for the rest of the day, there was no injury.

Later in the Ukraine, a bullet came even closer. Although he was in combat, he still hadn't thought of the enemy as his enemy.

Then a rumor began to circulate. They were headed to Stalingrad, a city barely hanging on by the Russian forces. The German army had since been joined by the Romanians and a few Italian units for this last push to finish off the capture of the city. Wally's group was going in to support the siege on the city, but first they had to get there.

The good roads were being used by the trucks and tanks while the men struggled on side roads and ditches. Walking took almost another month. Wagons brought the men food, although far from the quantity that they had received while on the train. No one explained why they couldn't have continued on by train and arrived weeks sooner.

Such was the fate of the foot soldier. First into the battle, but last to know the plans.

CHAPTER 14

THE RUSSIAN FRONT

As the ground troops pushed the Russians back, there was talk of their surrender to the invaders. It would have made sense. Many of the Russians who were captured professed hatred of Communism and of Joseph Stalin, but the German command gave no leniency.

Captured Russians were executed on the spot by the hundreds. Soon there were no surrenders, as the Russians knew the fate of such a move. They began fighting to the death, some committing suicide instead.

Finally, Wally saw a large river. He was told it was the Volga, the river that split the city of Stalingrad in two parts. The Germans were only on the west side. No forces had yet successfully crossed to the east bank.

Wally's unit made camp a few miles outside of Stalingrad. It was now October and the rains came. There was mud everywhere. Tanks ground to a halt. Trucks could not move. The attack settled into a stalemate. Gen. Paulus, commander of the Sixth Army, was seen by the troops on occasion, but little news was shared with the troops. Unknown to the units embedded in Stalingrad, Russian forces, instead of surrendering, began the encirclement of the German and Romanian forces.

After weeks, Wally's unit was ordered to enter the city. Most of its buildings were totally destroyed, first from the Luftwaffe bombs and then from the repeated artillery exchanges by both sides in earlier months.

Dead bodies were everywhere. Most had peasant clothing, as the bodies of German soldiers who had been killed were removed and buried. There was no one to bury the Russians.

The few buildings that remained standing were often filled with Russian soldiers and civilians who were fighting just as hard as the military troops to survive. Wally tried to just stay out of harm's way.

Before Stalingrad, Wally had never seen a large city other than Krakow. That Polish city was not damaged at all as the Germans took over his country. The utter destruction of Stalingrad was incredible. Wally wondered if a place so destroyed could ever be rebuilt. If the Germans were successful, Wally just might have to help in the rebuilding. Why would Hitler want this damaged city?

The German plan had envisioned that the Volga would be crossed by October and the entire city taken by early November. That just wasn't happening. The Russians, with their backs to the proverbial wall, were fighting for their very lives.

The weather was changing. Each day the temperature fell a degree or two and never came back. Food was restricted, rations were severely cut. Morale was dropping even faster than the temperature.

The troops were pushed to fully secure the west half of the city. Barges on the river often contained Russians with artillery shells that were lobbed onto the German troops with ferocity.

Wally's duty was to man a machine gun post at various locations. At other times, he and his fellow soldiers were required to search the abandoned buildings for snipers and deserters. These shellings were the most serious, although sniper fire was not far behind.

Wally made only one friend in the trek from Germany to the Stalingrad, Josef Korzeniowski. They rode, walked and froze together for months now. In early November, they were together on one occasion as their unit came under fire.

Artillery shells landed quite near Josef and Wally. A shell exploded by Josef. His body partially shielded Wally from the blast. Josef's blood now covered Wally. Pieces of Wally's clothing were torn away with the blast. He sank in shock, holding Josef as he died.

As the man died, Wally stayed at his side, and made a promise to himself. He would not befriend any more soldiers. It was too painful. Why befriend a man who would probably be dead within days? This was a new attitude for the friendly, helpful Polish boy of only months before.

Wally took some of Josef's clothing and added it to his own. His body was buried on the site of the confrontation with minimal respect. After all, the officers were German and Josef was a mere Pole.

As the first of December arrived, the food almost disappeared. Wally received one cup of wheat bran each day. The pounds fell off him. The cold drove all the troops to search out more clothing. When a comrade was killed, his jackets and boots were stripped from the body and worn by his fellow soldier, often full of blood and perhaps even body particulate. Wally had gotten an extra coat when his friend was killed.

The nationalities in the various companies were now completely mixed, as units suffered catastrophic losses. Wally was manning his machine gun about half of the time. The rest of the time he could do what he wanted. What he wanted, however, didn't amount to much. Warmth, food, a glass of beer and a heavier coat; however, these items just did not exist. So the troops went to their primitive shelters, got out of the wind and used their own body heat to warm the hole a few degrees. The days went by, but nothing changed except Wally's weight.

There was always limited manpower to guard the Russian prisoners and never enough food. So thousands of Russians who had surrendered were forced to go into the woods, dig their own graves and were then shot and thrown into the trenches.

Now, even fewer Russian troops surrendered. They logically decided that since they were going to die either way, they might as well die defending the motherland.

Wally knew little of international politics. The other men talked, saying that Hitler was making a big mistake with this policy of annihilation. Many of the Russian troops may well have joined the German forces to overthrow Stalin and the Kremlin, but that was not to be.

Wally, now inside Stalingrad itself, knew very little of the bigger picture of this historic battle. The German Sixth Army started its siege on August 23, under a plan known as Operation Barbarossa, when Wally was trudging across the Ukraine. Now it was winter. The Germans pushed the Soviet troops to the banks of the Volga River but were not able to cross it. This was an important river to the Soviets, as it was navigable when not frozen. The cost in the attempts to cross it was enormous. A thousand German soldiers died each day.

Wally was tired. There still were no new uniforms or winter clothing. At first the skirmishes with the Soviet troops were hit and miss. The biggest danger to German soldiers was the sniper. There were several renowned Russian snipers, the most famous of whom was Vasely Zaytsev, with 225 confirmed kills during the battle of Stalingrad. Some were not so famous but were still deadly. Wally and his men were in constant fear of these Russian snipers as the shots rang out from nowhere.

When November passed, the Soviets launched Operation Uranus, a two-pronged attack at the Romanian and Hungarian troops who were to protect the Sixth Army's flanks. The war was closing in on the Germans. By December, the entire German army was encircled by the Soviets. The encirclement was known as the Kessel, German for "cauldron."

What had been an impregnable line of German troops, from Leningrad on the north to Rostov on the south, had been broken. The few aircraft that survived a flight into Stalingrad were forced to land on narrow landing strips within the German occupied area. These planes were the only supply of food and ammunition. Both were running out. The empty aircraft also were the only means of evacuation for the wounded. The men now openly talked of the fact that they had been encircled. "The Kessel" was now complete.

One day, as Wally was checking out another abandoned building, he saw Gen. Paulus with a group of officers and enlisted troops.

"We are starving, General," said one soldier with more courage than intelligence. Gen. Paulus looked him straight on and replied, "I am starving as well. It will get better."

Wally could understand this German but knew better than to believe it.

The temperature fell below zero degrees Fahrenheit and the winds picked up velocity. It was so cold, Wally could hear the snow crack as he walked on it. While the abandoned buildings were used by some soldiers for shelter, most men had to construct shelter for themselves.

Wally's unit found several bomb craters, dragged downed trees and pieces of lumber from destroyed buildings and made a large covered fox hole. They created a diversion of the smoke from their fire so that they weren't an easy target for the Russian artillery. Their minimal gear was stored inside.

The forward movement of the crack German troops ground to a complete halt. The orders were to stay put. Retreat was out of the question for Hitler, and Paulus obeyed his orders, insane as they were. Germany had lost this campaign. Even the lowly ground troops now feared what might be ahead.

Although most of the buildings on the west side of the river were destroyed, Soviet troops fought on that month, moving from window to window, building to building.

One of Wally's early duties was to provide cover for German troops who were sweeping these bombed out buildings for snipers and pockets of Soviet resisters. It was deadly work.

The troops had received minimal food since early November. By now, there was talk among the men of a German surrender, even though Hitler had refused to believe that Soviet peasants could beat the crack German forces. Relief was being sent under a plan entitled "Operation Winter Storm" involving German tanks. The hope was to break the encirclement by December 19, but the German relief troops only got within 48 miles of the Kessel before being soundly defeated.

The date was now December 15, 1942. The Soviets had a new battle plan called "Operation Little Saturn." It was simple. The Soviet troops would punch a hole through the Italian troops on the north side of the Kessel and push in to the inner city. The Soviets were already retaking some of the suburbs. Russian civilians were fighting the German troops side by side with the Soviet troops.

The battle for Stalingrad would become the bloodiest battle ever fought in any war. Two million people were to die.

Wally started that day on sentry duty at his machine gun post with one other soldier. His shift lasted about six hours before he was relieved. His machine gun sat beside him, quiet but deadly.

Wally, to the best of his knowledge, had never killed a Soviet. He had no desire to kill. He had no grudge against the Russians. When he had to fire, he aimed over the heads of the enemy.

Wally spent the rest of the day inside the hut with three other men. None were well known to him. They were clearly German. His German was somewhat better, but he made no attempt at conversation. He just curled up in a ball and tried to stay warm enough to at least sleep a few hours.

The situation was unbearable. They were all going to freeze to death, be captured and killed by the Soviets or get shot by a sniper going to and from their posts.

Wally had a lot of time to think. Who would have imagined what had happened to his life since September 1939? In just three years he had seen the horrors of Auschwitz, including the total domination of a people by an opposing force, had military training in a language he didn't really speak, and had taken a brutal train ride across the Steppe.

Now he was in a battle in which the largest and most powerful enemy was not necessarily the Soviet army but Mother Nature herself.

He had to believe that this was the German plan for him. His minimal training, his inadequate clothing and his lack of food all seemed to say to him that night that the Germans just planned for him to die. Perhaps all of the Polish draftees were meant to die. Then there would be more room for the Germans to move into his country. Perhaps this was the plan for the Jews and the gypsies. Just kill them and make more room for the pure Aryan race. He fell asleep.

CHAPTER 15

SURRENDERING TO GOD AND BATTLE WOUNDS

The next day, December 16, Wally was quartered in the hole in the ground with tree branches and boards propped across it to create a partial roof. Wally's entire daily ration was still one cup of wheat. Melted snow was the only source of water. Wally had lost more than 20 pounds.

Except for some jackets he had taken from dead German soldiers, his clothing consisted of the same summer uniform he had in September. His entire body was infested with lice.

The temperature was now well below zero every day. Because he had taken articles of clothing from dead German soldiers, he was now wearing three jackets but only a thin pair of gloves, and his boots were summer issue. Everyone was underdressed and underfed.

It was clear that some terrible end was approaching. Morale was low. Soldiers were being shot by their own sergeants and officers for disobedience, cowardice or just refusal to stand up or salute. Germany was losing this battle.

Christmas was but a week away. Shortly after midnight, Wally left the protection of the bunker to make his way to a machine gun post for his six-hour watch with another Polish soldier he knew only as Erich. He was freezing and hungry. Several hours passed as he contemplated his future. No replacement had shown up as was supposed to happen.

He waited … and then he just broke.

Looking up, Wally asked God to just take him, yelling his Polish request into the night sky. Wally then turned to his bunker, leaving Erich behind. He knew his sergeant was inside. He also knew that he could be shot for any minor infraction of orders, let alone desertion.

Walking off one's post was certainly a deadly offense, but tonight Wally Pieszka did not care.

He entered the bunker feet first, sliding down into the hole. There were five men inside, huddled together. Wally's sergeant, a man named Weiss, immediately asked him why he had left his post. Wally made no reply.

"Do you want to be shot? Get your ass out of here and go back to your watch!" Sgt. Weiss yelled. Wally continued to sit.

There was no wind. The temperature in the bunker was near zero, a far improvement over the outside. The sergeant continued with his berating. When it was apparent that Sgt. Weiss was preparing to pull his pistol and shoot him, Wally arose, pulled himself out of the bunker and started back to his post to join Erich.

As he trudged back to his post, Wally wondered what had just happened. What had made him change his mind and go back to his post? Was his will to survive that strong or was the brief break in the warmer air enough to make him reconsider joining God as his alternative?

No man knows his ultimate breaking point until he faces it, and Wally was no different. In spite of the terrible conditions and being stationed somewhere beyond a man's comprehension, Wally was a survivor.

Did his decision come from his religion, his childhood or his determined character? That night, Wally went from a passive soldier to a man who would beat these odds. He didn't quite know how yet, but going back to his post was a start.

Wally had no time to ponder anything further while he walked from the bunker. Just then, an explosion ripped through the air.

A Russian artillery shell landed on the bunker he had just vacated. Instantly he felt pain in his right knee.

He was knocked by the concussion into a snow-filled ditch. The five men he had just left were probably all dead. He knew his company was gone.

He was woozy and the pain was incredible. Wally was losing blood and there was a hunk of shrapnel lodged in his knee. He began to lose consciousness from the ordeal and welcomed the slip into a place where there was no more pain.

Was he dying? For a moment, he contemplated his situation. Were his days of fighting for Germany on the Russian front over for now? Would he survive this night in a snow-filled ditch?

Unknown to Wally and most of the men, the Kessel encircled the 265,000 German, Italian, Hungarian and Romanian troops. They were now trapped inside. As these forces were pushed back, there was fear that the airfields, the life blood of survival, might be lost. Paulus was losing his precious few supplies he had been receiving through these aircraft. But none of this mattered to Wally as he passed out.

He lay in a ravine, on his back. His head was spinning. He realized that his knee was seriously injured. In spite of the cold, he lifted his head to look at his wound, but there wasn't enough light to see. He could feel wetness on his pant leg by his right knee. The pain's intensity caused him to pass out again.

Over the next six hours, Wally was conscious for only a few moments. He wondered if he could get up, but each time he tried he would pass out. When he was conscious, he didn't think about dying or living. He just wanted to get up from that snow-filled ditch.

He knew he was bleeding, but he had no idea how much.

Finally, he let himself sleep with a last thought that this might be better than living after all.

It was just before dawn on December 17, 1943. Wally did not know that the entire German army would surrender within a few weeks, and some units within two days.

Wally was not going to be one of them. He started believing that he was going to be one of the last battle deaths of the Stalingrad campaign. Hundreds of thousands of Germans and Romanians who did surrender would be summarily executed when captured, or die in Russian prison camps.

As it had happened years before, another European power would lose again trying to subdue a Russian city. Had Napoleon not learned his lesson at Moscow the century before? No other country had ever won a war deep in Russia in the winter.

As he lay there, Wally knew nothing of Napoleon, Moscow or any other history. Was death just hours away? Was the life of Wladyslaw Pieszka at an end, or would some miracle intervene and let this young man live a bit longer?

A miracle happened when the men in the bunker were brought their meager rations and he was found missing. A search found Wally unconscious in the ditch.

CHAPTER 16

THE MEDICAL TENT

Wally lay semiconscious in the ditch for almost eight hours before a fellow soldier discovered him. Placed on a stretcher, he was taken to the field hospital, a mere tent in the middle of the snowy landscape.

There were no beds in this scant medical facility. The wounded, including Wally, lay on two rows of straw spread throughout the tent.

There were a few doctors who walked the narrow seam between the two rows. The doctors were overworked and totally understaffed for the number of injuries taking place every hour of the day and night.

Eventually, a doctor attended to his leg, removing some of the metal and placing a full leg brace on him. He lay in the straw for the night. There was no medicine to relieve the pain, and the leg throbbed the entire next day.

Wally couldn't tell if he was awake or asleep. He kept losing consciousness and then jerking awake. He thought about the night before and the artillery shell. He realized those men in the bunker were surely dead. But Wally had seen so much carnage, this was just one more event in this crazy winter. He went back to a hazy sleep.

When he awoke, he realized that there was some minimal heat inside the tent. It was above zero, the warmest surroundings he had "enjoyed" in days. He could now hear moaning most of the time and then realized that he was one of those moaning.

It was getting colder as night approached and there were no real blankets. He had something covering him but he had no idea what it was. It smelled and was stiff, but it helped warm him a bit. None of his clothing had been removed, save his right pant leg. All the wounded still had on their uniforms and jackets. Time went slowly.

As he lay there freezing, Wally wondered what his next fate in life might be. Was he to die here at the age of nineteen? He had never been with a woman, had never graduated from painting school or even grade school, and really never had a job that he had chosen. His family was thousands of miles away, living under a foreign enemy, struggling daily for survival themselves in their very own home. He thought of his mother, his father and his three half-brothers.

Where were they now? Frank was probably home making parts

for the German Army, so he was safe. Who knew what was happening with Emil? Was he still a prisoner of war or had the Germans just taken him out and shot him to preserve food? Andrew was at home four months ago. Who could know where he was now? Had he been forced into the German Army or was the tuberculosis trick still working?

Wally was able to calculate that he had been unconscious at least twelve hours, as it was now dark. The fact that he didn't have frostbite was a miracle. He could feel all the parts of his body and was able to raise his head for a bit to look around.

He could make out two distinct rows of wounded soldiers. The center aisle was made of wooden planks to keep the medical personnel from walking in the mud. The two rows of straw were totally filled with men. He saw no empty spaces and noticed the wounded were within only inches from each other. There were no beds. He saw a few men, perhaps doctors, wandering among the dozens of wounded soldiers. Most were quiet; a few praying.

Wally did not remember being brought to the tent, but it seemed safe for now. The pain was still intense, mostly at his knee. His head hurt as well, probably from the concussion of the artillery shell. He remembered only seeing the explosion, feeling the impact and then the searing pain in his knee. He had no specific comprehension of the time he lay in the ditch. He believed it was the night before, but who knew for sure?

He again recalled the sergeant and the men in the dugout. While they were fellow troops, he still had no feeling of loss. They were almost completely unknown to him. He thought of his one friend, a Polish man from a neighboring village. They had struck up a friendship on the walk to Stalingrad. They spoke Polish when no one was around. They even joked. But that all changed a few weeks ago when his friend caught the impact of an explosion with his body. In a matter of a few minutes, his friend's eyes rolled back into his head and he was gone. This was the only soldier for whom Wally had any feeling, any compassion, any caring.

As he lay in pain on the straw, he was still being eaten by lice and wondered what possibly could be next. Would it be even worse? Wally had heard that when a neighboring wounded patient died and the body cooled, his lice would leave and find the nearest living body. He hoped that the wounded soldiers on either side of him would live through the next day or so for that reason alone.

As he thought these wretched thoughts, the roar of an approaching airplane filled the air.

The sound of machine gun fire filled the quiet air. Bullets began ripping through the canvas tent and into the right side of the hospital. Men screamed. Others ducked for cover, of which there was none. Some of the standing doctors fell. The straw on the right side of the tent flew into the air.

In the modest lighting inside the tent, Wally could see the bullets striking straw and people. The wounded and the doctors were in a complete panic.

Clearly, most of the men on the right side were dead. Yet the men on his side of the aisle were untouched. What to do?

Wally had seen enough of the Russians. These pilots were unmerciful. This one would be back and Wally's left side would be the next target. He had to get out of there.

He tried his leg and was able to lift himself off the straw, but he was bent over. He couldn't put any weight on his right leg to stand up straight, let alone walk. He was trapped.

No one seemed to be trying to get out of the tent, as though this frail piece of canvas could protect them. Wally knew better. He had to move. Behind his head was a piece of wood. It did not seem to belong there. Perhaps it was for a bottle of blood, but it was there! Wally was able to lean over far enough to grab the stick. It was about a four feet long and looked sturdy. It might make a crutch.

With the stick under his right shoulder, Wally was able to finally extricate himself from the straw and into the narrow aisle. There were two men writhing in front of him. They appeared to be part of the medical staff. There were a dozen or so men who were screaming out in pain and begging for help, to no avail.

Wally knew he couldn't help anyone; he could barely move himself. Each step was wracked with pain. He began to feel light-headed again. He made it as far as the front flap of the tent, but it was tied shut to keep the wind from blowing in.

Just then, someone in front of him tore the flap away and headed out into the cold December night. Wally followed him as best he could. He made it no more than 50 feet when he collapsed into a snow bank by the path leading into the hospital tent. He couldn't move.

Wally laid there for a while. No one seemed to come or go along the path. No fighter plane returned to finish the job on the hospital tent.

Wally could not rise. He again contemplated his death. He could be flung into a hole with dozens of other dead German soldiers, perhaps many from the hospital tent just behind him. Perhaps this was to be his demise. Time would tell, but time was clearly running out for Wally Pieszka. Had his time come?

"What is this? He is alive. He has the red tag."

Someone was talking near him. It was in German but simple enough that Wally could understand.

"You are a lucky man, Private. We are going to save your life. We are the crew of the plane right over there and we have room for you."

Wally didn't speak a word. His accent would have let the German airmen know he wasn't a German, and they would surely continue looking for a pure German soldier to save. He nodded his understanding.

The two airmen lifted Wally to a standing position. Even in the night they could see and feel the long brace on Wally's leg. They lifted him by the shoulders and began moving away from the hospital tent. Fortunately, the landing strip was near the medical tent.

The walk required some weight on his legs and the pain was intense. He moaned a bit and bit his lip, mindful not to say any words. They walked a hundred yards before Wally saw the airplane. It was in the dark end of what appeared to be an open field. The lights around the field were off, probably to avoid making the airplane more of a target for the Russian fighters. It had a single propeller and a door halfway down the side. The tail had a swastika painted on it. Wally could see no guns protruding from the sides or front as they approached the door.

Wally was lifted into the plane by the two airmen and helped by a third man inside. He could see three hammocks hanging from the ceiling of the plane, one above the other. They gently put Wally in the bottom hammock and turned back to the door. The two men who found him exited the aircraft, leaving the one man inside the plane.

Unknown to Wally, this was an airplane designed to carry everything. Germany built almost three thousand of these versatile airplanes, called Storches, during the war. They were created for short takeoffs and landings and could literally land on a city street. These single engine airplanes were used in Russia, Africa, Finland and France. The Storch was used in 1943 to slip Mussolini out of Italy after its fall to Allied Forces.

"I am your pilot. We will wait until dark to fly out. If we can sneak out before morning, we have a good chance of beating the Russian fighters. We will fly about three or four hours to a place called Limonskia. It is still in Russia, but we control the airport there." Wally understood most of what the pilot had said and nodded to him.

With that, the pilot returned to the front of the plane. Wally heard more noise outside the plane and soon the two airmen returned with two more wounded soldiers. Each displayed the important red tag. They were to be evacuated. They were lifted into the upper two hammocks and all three of them were secured with webbing so that they would not fall out.

Soon, Wally heard an engine start to turn over. It took a few seconds but finally caught. The pilot took his time revving the engine, letting it warm up sufficiently in this Russian freezer to permit him to fly out of this hell-hole. One of the airmen was clearly the co-pilot and took his seat at the controls. The third airman buckled up in a jump seat on the right side of the plane as it began to taxi.

CHAPTER 17

THE FLIGHT OUT

This was all new to Wally. He had never been near an airplane, let alone flown in one. The only planes he had seen were high in the sky over him as his troops moved from one location to another. So, as this 19-year-old boy pondered his knee, his first airplane flight and his future, the small plane headed west, leaving the horrendous scene at Stalingrad behind.

Wally had escaped a disaster. He had just personally survived the bloodiest battlefield in the history of warfare.

The Sixth Army collapsed the following month. More than 100,000 German and Axis soldiers surrendered and were taken into Russian custody. Of that number, only 6,000 would live to see the end of the war and repatriation.

Stalingrad was destroyed. The Russian army at Stalingrad was almost completely annihilated. Civilian casualties ran into the hundreds of thousands. Wally's survival by the chance of being flown out on December 18, 1942, was 1 in 100,000 of the troops still stationed in Stalingrad that December day.

The airfield lasted only six more days. Flights both in and out ended. No more supplies were received and no more wounded soldiers were evacuated. The end was inevitable, but Hitler insisted that Gen. Paulus stay there. He would not permit a retreat. Paulus was a soldier, and he obeyed.

The airplane's engine sounded as though it was slowing down. Wally had slept for most of the flight, but the change in the noise awakened him for his first landing. He was still in his German uniform. The doctors had merely sliced open his pant leg for the medical attention. There were no hospital gowns and no blankets to be spared. Wally shivered in his uniform and coats.

The airplane bumped hard against the ground several times before it began to slow down. The pressure sent pain shooting through his knee. Wally was the first patient to be removed from the plane. He was carried to an abandoned school house converted into a makeshift hospital. Again, there were no beds, just straw on the ground. No one offered food or water right away. Wally's mouth was dry. Finally an attendant came over with a bottle of water and held it to his lips. Wally drank deeply.

"You are here only for a short time. There is another airplane that will take more of you out of Russia to a real hospital," said the attendant.

Wally could understand his German quite easily, as though it was the attendant's second language as well. After the water, Wally fell back asleep.

He was awakened by movement. He was being put on a stretcher and carried to another airplane, this one much larger than the first. Wally was placed on the floor of the airplane along with a couple of dozen other wounded men. They were not secured in any way, but were placed next to each other to help alleviate movement. Soon, the now familiar noise of a revving engine filled the interior of the airplane as the plane began to taxi.

Wally held on the best he could, but he bumped into the men beside him during the takeoff. Again, no one spoke to anyone else. Once in the air, there was nothing left to do but sleep.

During the flight, Wally noticed a new phenomenon. He would awake from his slumber with a jerk, his mind racing through fire, explosions and pain. He would shake for several minutes. This was unlike anything he had experienced before. He had no idea what was the cause of these new images, but they caused immediate and overwhelming fear in him.

Wally had never felt these emotions before. The half-dreams and half-nightmares were new to him. He tried to sleep, but the thoughts wouldn't quit and he couldn't make them disappear.

After several hours, the big airplane started its descent. Again, the bumpy landing caused more pain to Wally's knee. Soon, the airplane stopped and the door on the side was opened. A group of attendants entered the plane and began removing the wounded men. Wally was the last to be removed from the plane. He had no idea where he was. German was spoken all around him.

Wally was carried on a stretcher to an ambulance. The ride to the hospital took no more than 20 minutes. He could see that the building was old, but it seemed in good repair, and it had heat.

He was taken to a room without beds. It was more like an examination room. A large German woman with rubber gloves began removing every piece of Wally's clothing. When she got to his undershorts, Wally put his hands in front of his private parts, and she laughed. "What you got under there, my little man, something you are so proud of?"

With that she opened a large canister and took what looked like white paste from a jar. Wally was now pushed up against a table totally nude. The nurse started smearing the white contents of the jar all over his body, under his arms, in the crack of his behind, his chest, his legs and even all over his genitals.

"It kills those lice that you have all over your body, young man. It will burn a bit but the lice will all die." And they did.

Whatever the concoction, not only did it kill the lice, it destroyed most of the body hair along with them. Wally never grew back all of the hair he lost that day. His armpits and chest hair would be minimal after that paste.

After this embarrassing ordeal was finished, Wally was taken to a room with several beds, where he would remain the rest of the day.

At dawn on December 21, 1942, Wally was taken to another room and given anesthesia. He later learned that a surgeon had opened his knee and removed a large fragment of shrapnel. When he awoke, he could hear two nurses at the door of his room speaking Polish.

"Where am I?" he asked the women in Polish.

"Krakow, you Swabia." (A Polish word for low class foreigners.) With that, they walked away. They thought him to be German, but he was home in Poland. He had survived the Russian Front.

What was coming next? He was still seriously wounded and the jerking and cringing he experienced on the second plane flight continued. Would they treat him and send him back to Russia?

He had a cast from his ankle to his upper thigh. It was uncomfortable and it itched, although this irritation was nothing compared to the lice that were now gone.

Food started to come and it was good. The attendants were kind. Wally did not broadcast his nationality except to the two Polish nurses, but all the wounded were apparently heroes, even those who weren't German. War propaganda insisted that they be treated well, having faced the Russians.

Wally was being treated better than he had been treated since leaving home to paint at Auschwitz. But would it last?

It was almost Christmas. Where would he spend Christmas? Tomorrow was the 22nd.

CHAPTER 18

HIS RECOVERY

The doctors had done all they could do with the shrapnel wound to Wally's right knee. There were no x-rays, just probing and feeling. They told Wally that it was removed and he should expect a complete recovery.

Wally, however, was nowhere near ready for combat or a return to his unit. There had to be physical rehabilitation. The nurses noted in his medical records that patient Pieszka was prone to waking up in the middle of the night screaming. He seemed traumatized and often shook for minutes after being awakened.

With those notes in his medical records, Wally was placed on a train for Wiesbaden, Germany. He made the trip on a stretcher, as he could not yet walk. The train took the wounded from Poland back to Germany.

These were the heroes of the campaign. The officials spared no expense to use this opportunity for propaganda purposes. The returning men were to be treated royally. In fact, Private Pieszka would soon be Corporal Pieszka.

The train was immaculate. Wally's stretcher was placed near one of the train windows. He thought how different the accommodations were from the "cattle" train that took him to Russia just five months ago. Those five months seemed like a lifetime. A dozen other wounded men were on the train car with various injuries. Some could move around, but some were confined to stretchers and wheel chairs.

Wally could not erase the memories of Stalingrad from his mind. Even though he had been issued a completely new wardrobe, his memories of the cold, the filth and the danger permeated his mind.

His clothes were now clean. At least the paste had killed the lice. Meals were brought to his stretcher by an aide and the food was good. Except for the excruciating pain in his knee, life was as good as it had been for months, but he was sad and scared.

As the train made its way across Poland, Wally realized that it was again passing close to his home through Chybie. A neighbor of the Pieszka family was in Chybie that very day and believed that he saw Wally through the train window as the train stopped at the station for a few moments. The neighbor later told the family he believed Wally had a leg missing.

Christmas was coming, yet there would be no home-cooked meal or the joy of a family around him. Had he known the word depression, he would have realized how deeply he had retreated into his mind and was shutting out the world around him. While he was glad to be alive, he could not stop wondering about what would come next.

The train arrived in Wiesbaden on December 22, 1942. The men were taken by trucks to the military hospital. Wally was placed in a room with three other soldiers. All had been seriously wounded. There wasn't much talking. Doctors and nurses came and went, but there was minimal discussion with the patients. The nurses spoke German, but two had distinct accents. Wally wondered where they were from.

On the second day, December 23, 1942, Wally was informed that his parents would be coming the next day for a visit. It would be Christmas Eve. He wondered how they would get to Germany and how they could afford it. But for the first time in months, he smiled.

The next day, Wally's parents arrived. They had not been informed of the seriousness of Wally's injuries, only that he needed hospitalization. As soon as his mother entered the room, she grabbed Wally's right knee and squeezed, perhaps showing a mother's love for her son or perhaps confirming that the neighbor was wrong that Wally had lost a leg. He quickly wished it had been the other knee.

In spite of the pain, the next four days were a joy. His parents were able to stay in the hospital while they visited their son. Wally's mother contracted a terrible cold but was undaunted. She would stay by her son as long as permitted.

His parents and he spoke German at first, but soon quietly lapsed into Polish. The words sounded so good and were so easily understood after months of his struggling with German words and phrases. Visits were about an hour long, and then they would be asked to leave because their son needed rest. Each time, Wally feared that this would be the last visit. His distrust of the word of the German officials continued.

For the first time in months, there was connection with home. His parents quickly outlined life in Ilownica. Frank now had a child. He was working in his former capacity as a tool and die maker, still producing needed war material. As such, he was an essential civilian with no risk of being drafted. Frank was living near his parents and could see them quite often.

Emil was still a prisoner of war. His wife, Sophia, had been notified of his capture and confinement at the time, but no further word was forthcoming. She and their child, Janek, still lived with Wally's parents and would for the balance of the war.

Andrew remained a civilian. He had met and married a woman named Mary Kichitia. They lived in her home in a neighboring village. How long Andrew could stay out of the German draft was unknown, and was a definite worry to Wally's mother. Wally was enough. She could not bear another son being forced to be a German soldier. Her village constantly received word that other local men drafted into the German army had been killed. She already spent the better part of last year worrying about Wally.

After Christmas, Wally's parents made their way home. His mother had become quite ill and had received some medication from the hospital. The separation was made bearable by a promise that upon his discharge from the hospital, Wally would be permitted to spend some time at home before his next assignment.

Rehabilitation was slow and the wound stayed tender. The nurses who were, in fact, Polish themselves, saw the medical report of the mental state of their patient on his arrival. They noted additional findings of nightmares and panic. There was a fluctuation in his temperature as well.

The reports may have been exaggerated a bit as the two nurses realized that Wally also was Polish. There was a bit of special care for him when they were on duty. They quietly talked and confirmed that they, too, were from Silesia. There was a nun, who also attended to Wally at times. She spoke perfect German, but once heard Wally praying in Polish. She said, "Lez Bogiem. Go with God." Wally asked if she was Polish and she responded that she was, but did not speak to Wally in Polish again.

After two months of physical therapy, the nun came to Wally and told him, "We and the doctors believe that you have a fairly serious mental condition. There is a special therapy that appears to help with the stress and sadness you have, and it may help with the nightmares. It involves low levels of electricity being run through your body. It will not harm you and may help to calm you down."

Wally had not heard of such a treatment, but one of the nurses told him quietly in Polish, "At best, it will calm you down, but even if it doesn't work all that well, the therapy will take about 60 days and you will not be returned to active duty until it is over."

Based on some of the rumors about the retreat from the Russian Front, this seemed like a gift from heaven. Still, Wally wondered how much it would hurt.

In early March, 1943, Wally started this new treatment. He was taken to a special room and seated in a wooden chair. He was handed two metal handles with wires protruding from each end. He was told to sit quietly and soon electric current would start to run to the handles. The instruction came from a middle-aged woman in civilian clothes. She did not give her name nor ask Wally for his. She told him merely to hold the handles and keep his feet, which were now bare, on the metal plate in front of his seat.

Soon Wally could feel a shock running through his body. It started in his feet and extended to his arms. His chest would tighten and his muscles would contract. Then the current would lessen and his whole body relaxed. This was then repeated a dozen or more times. The shock was uncomfortable but not painful. He would then return to his hospital room.

This "dry" treatment, as Wally would learn, was repeated every other day for ten treatments. Then the scene changed. When Wally entered the room, there was a basin of water about a foot deep. He again sat in the wooden chair but now, as he held the two handles, he was to immerse his elbows in the basin of water. The sensation was different. Again, there really wasn't any pain, but it felt like something was crawling all over his body. There were ten treatments spread over twenty days with the water basin. Wally was feeling a bit better and was not shouting at night any more.

The third round of shock therapy followed immediately. Now the treatment changed dramatically. As Wally entered this room, there was no chair, only a tub of water filled to the top. Wally was told to enter the water completely nude. There was a ledge where he could partially sit, so the water went up to his neck. He was to lie back. Again the electrical current passed through him, starting slowly and then increasing. This time he felt as though ants were marching up and down his back. There was no pain, but the feeling like insects running all over him was disturbing.

Each time he was finished with a session, a doctor would check his reflexes and ask a few questions. Wally answered as best he could in German and would go back to his room. His official diagnosis was that he had a nerve disturbance.

The final round of treatments was again a total of ten times spread over twenty days. He was glad to be done with this round of electricity. His knee was quite a bit better, and by the end of April, he was declared fit to return to duty. He was being sent back to his unit at Saarbrucken. First, however, there was the long anticipated leave.

Wally arrived by train and was met by his family in Chybie. He couldn't believe how good his home looked. He had a room and a bed in the family house. The big news was that Andrew had been drafted and was gone, but his sister-in-law, Sophia, and her baby were there. After the places Wally had been, having a bedroom to himself was incredible. The meals were scrumptious and the conversation never stopped. Most of the time was spent in his home.

The small farm still produced enough that the family had food.

Wally took walks into town. He again inquired quietly of Regina, but no one had any new news on her family's disappearance. A German family was operating the store. Such things were happening everywhere to Jewish families. Wally made no comment and walked home with sadness. After what he had seen in Auschwitz, he had a pretty good idea what had happened to his friend and her family.

Andrew's wife was called Mary. Since his being drafted, Mary and his parents heard from Andrew a couple of times but were never told where he was. Emil's wife was still present in the home but she seemed depressed and reserved. Most likely she had wished for a different son to return home. That was not to be, as Emil spent the rest of the war in the German prison camp. Each wife quietly struggled on.

Wally's mother was more emotional and showed her feelings quite often in the privacy of her home. Four sons. One in prison and two now in the active service of the German army. How much could a mother stand?

The days passed quickly and soon it was time to return to his base in Saarbrucken. Only his father accompanied him to the Chybie train station. They hugged and kissed each other's cheeks and Wally boarded the train.

The next forced interruption of his life was commencing. He was not to see his father again for many years.

CHAPTER 19

OFF TO ITALY

Wally arrived the next day at the camp in Saarbrucken and reported to his unit. He was escorted to a barracks, but not the one he had before when in training. This barracks had seasoned soldiers, not recruits. As he entered and was shown a bunk, the other soldiers merely watched. No one rose to meet him or welcome him. All wore German uniforms, but they could have been any nationality.

Wally was told when and where to report the next day. He found the mess hall and had supper. When he returned to the barracks, some men were in bed, but a few were talking, in German, of course. Although he had not spoken German very well at the first of his service, he was now able to understand quite a few words and phrases when they were spoken.

There was talk that his unit might be sent to Yugoslavia to fight the partisans. There were two distinct partisan groups who didn't get along and had no trust of the other, but both had the same mission -- to harass the German occupation forces. The largest partisan group was led by Tito and was considered a deadly enemy of the German troops. It seemed to Wally to be a very dangerous place. He went to bed thinking about Stalingrad and now Yugoslavia. Another death trap?

The next morning, Wally was told to assemble with other troops and get on a truck. The truck with a dozen men drove a short distance. In the back of the truck with the men were various tools, including axes and two-man saws. They were dropped off near a large pile of wooden timbers. These trees had been rough-cut but not finished. The assignment was to make lumber for new barracks, and the manual labor was being done by Italian political prisoners. Wally was to guard them, not necessarily to help them. The work was the same for the next two weeks.

One morning upon arriving at the sawing location, Wally was informed by the officer in charge that today these logs were to be sawn at an angle for roof rafters. He was part of a crew that was sawing the various logs into the desired length and width. Several men picked up the two-man saws and made their way to the lumber. Crude saw horses were available and the men indicated that Wally should grab a piece of timber and put it on the saw horses.

He grabbed one of the nearest timbers and placed it on a pair of the saw horses and stepped back. The job was the same as he had done for days now. The two men determined the place of the cut and began drawing the saw back and forth to create an angle on one end.

The timber immediately began to move on the saw horses. Wally stepped in, placing his hands on the timber to steady it. With that, the men took a long stroke with the saw. As they did, the blade came out of the groove and landed on Wally's right hand.

Blood was everywhere and the pain was immediate. Wally fell to the ground grasping his right hand.

German words filled the air, as several men rushed to his aid. It was clear that Wally's index finger was almost completely severed. Two men grabbed rags and tried to staunch the bleeding. One of the men yelled something and another man started the truck that Wally had come in.

Two men helped lead Wally to the truck. He got in, now grasping the finger and the rag as the blood continued to dribble on his pants. The first stop was the sick bay located quite near his barracks. A nurse and what might have been a doctor took Wally.

Wally was aware that he had to insist that the injury was not intentional, or the men who had cut him might have been shot.

The doctor dismissed them before removing the dirty rag to examine the wound as best he could. The blood continued to flow. The nurse wiped away as much of the blood as she could as the doctor prepared to stitch the wound closed.

The doctor sewed and Wally flinched. There was no shot to lessen the pain. As he peeked, Wally could see the bone inside the cut. It was deep. He tried to count the number of stitches the doctor used, but he felt woozy and lost track.

When the doctor was finished sewing, the nurse again cleaned the hand and the doctor placed a soft cast over the finger and got a sling for his right arm. He stated a number of things to Wally, but the words were long and unfamiliar to him. He understood none of it other than he was going next to the hospital on the camp.

The truck took Wally to the hospital and he was led to a bed. The thought of being wounded again and lying in a hospital with other wounded men reminded him of that awful night in Stalingrad on the straw hearing the Russian fighter coming in for its pass with machine guns blazing.

Wally awoke the next day and noticed that everyone was working at a normal pace. There were no panicked medical personnel running through the halls from one patient to the next. While there were several other patients in his room, the medical staff moved from one patient to the next carefully taking time with each of them. Wally felt much more comfortable. This place was far from the danger of war. But where and when would he go next? Yugoslavia?

Wally stayed in the hospital for three days and was then released back to his unit with certain restrictions. There weren't too many jobs he could handle in this position. Besides, he had just about severed his trigger finger. What good would he do with a rifle? Perhaps his days in the infantry were numbered.

At the end of the week, Wally knew two things. First, he was still in his sling and therefore not capable of being an active-duty infantryman. Second, his unit was shipping out for Yugoslavia, just as the rumor mill had predicted, but Wally was to remain in Saarbrucken.

He watched the men in his barracks pack their duffels with their belongings and exit the building into waiting trucks. He had very mixed emotions. He should have been going as a member of his unit. On the other hand, he knew the rumors of the dangers facing the partisans in Yugoslavia.

Once again, a freak incident had changed the course of Wally's history.

After two weeks, Wally was ordered to report to a sergeant in the next building. He entered what appeared to be a set of administrative offices. He and another man were waiting to be told to enter one of the offices. They both stood. The seated sergeant informed them of their orders. Wally could make out only some of the words.

He knew that it concerned some parts for artillery guns. He heard the words Italy and railroad. He understood that he and this other man were to accompany something on a train from Saarbrucken to somewhere in Italy. With that, they were handed some papers and dismissed.

Fortunately, the other man understood German well and Wally could just follow along. At the terminal was an assembled train with dozens of rail cars; some enclosed, some tankers and some open gondola types with shiny steel pieces on them.

Wally packed his belongings once again before leaving the barracks. He had no idea how long he would be gone. A soldier at the train took the two of them to the middle of the train where two open cars were loaded with pieces of metal. It became clear that these two cars were the substance of their assignment and were to be guarded night and day until delivered. Wally was able to learn that the cars would be transferred from train to train along the way, but they would always stay with these two cars.

Wally and the other man, who had never given his name, climbed up on the alternate ends of the two rail cars. They would have no relief, no beds and only the food that they brought or could buy at various stations along the way. Wally had a few extra deutschmarks and brought all of them with him. The train started to roll and Wally settled in.

Over the next few days, the train made slow progress. Often they were put on a siding as trains with apparently higher priority sped down the single set of tracks. At one point, they were uncoupled from the train and left on the siding alone. Since there were no toilet facilities, each man would walk a few feet away from the rail cars to relieve himself. It was even more primitive than the early years of his life in Poland.

There were two more switches of trains, and the days became two weeks. It was clear that they had gone through Rome and were headed even further south. There was talk in camp about the Americans and the British possibly making a landing on Sicily. Wally only knew that Sicily was an island to the west of Italy and not that far from the shore. Maybe what they were carrying was meant to help defeat any invasion of Italy.

Just before Naples, Wally's fellow soldier became deathly ill and couldn't stop vomiting. On one stop just past Rome, a German officer who approached the stopped train realized how sick this man was, and he allowed him to leave the train. Wally was told that he would complete the mission and deliver the metal objects alone. There he learned that they had something to do with artillery guns. They looked like shields, not something that was used to fire big guns.

After Naples, the train went to Reggio di Calabria where it finally stopped. German officials boarded the train and eventually came across the two rail cars that Wally was protecting. Perhaps that was a silly word because Wally merely had a pistol at his side and a finger that could not fit inside the trigger opening.

Wally heard that this place was near the northeast tip of Sicily and that if there were to be an invasion of Sicily, the crossing point into Italy would come at Reggio di Calabria. Apparently, this was why the Germans thought the place needed the material that Wally was delivering.

In slow German, one of the Germans laughed sardonically and said, "Great. We are shipping shields for our artillery guns, but they haven't sent us the guns themselves." Wally said nothing, but he wondered what was happening to the well-oiled, well-disciplined German army. Sending parts for a weapon that didn't exist seemed like a fairly supreme waste of time, energy and manpower.

The officer signed Wally's papers indicating that the shields had been received and indicated that Wally would be taking public train transportation back to his base. He gave Wally a two-day pass in Rome. Wally boarded a train that headed north. In a few hours, he was in Rome, but more importantly to a Catholic boy, the home of the Vatican. That was a place he wanted to see.

Wally was directed to German headquarters and took a bus from the train station to the base, which was located near the center of the city. He reported in, showed his papers and was assigned a room. The base had nothing but German soldiers; no Italians or civilians. The sergeant who checked him in told him he could spend two nights and then he would have to be off for his home base.

Wally contemplated whether there was any way to escape his enforced military duty. He understood that desertion meant death. He wondered if the Vatican could give him some sort of asylum.

Even though his German was poor, Wally heard that others made a similar escape. Did he have the courage to try this? Thanks to his injured hand, he had been getting some fairly safe duty. If he deserted, he couldn't go home. They would come for him just as they had for Andrew, and the family could not possibly be that lucky again.

Wally went to the mess hall and had a late lunch. He sat with no one, but listened to other men talking. One of the subjects was the Vatican. He listened as carefully as he could. It seemed that the Vatican had stated a position to the Germans that it had no way to house and keep people seeking asylum. They mentioned that such people, whether deserters or civilians, were eventually turned over to the German army.

Wally could not tell if what he heard was true or merely a rumor. He decided that he would have to be very careful. He would look for someone inside the Vatican who was speaking Polish. He knew no Italian, and unless Latin phrases he learned in church were being spoken, he was out of luck.

The trip to the Vatican required civilian clothes, and Wally had none. The same sergeant who checked him in explained that one could rent civilian clothing for such a visit. Wally found the clothing room, paid his deutschmarks and received some well-worn, ill-fitting pants and a shirt. He put his uniform on his bed, made the change, and headed out the door to find a bus for the Vatican. He quickly realized that the Vatican was quite a long way from the German headquarters, so he rethought his plan and returned to the base. The Vatican would have to wait another day. Instead, he put his uniform back on and strolled through the center area of Rome.

Wally awoke early the next morning, had a fast breakfast at the mess hall and headed out. He now knew the number of the bus to take him near Vatican City. Wally entered the Vatican in total awe. He had never seen anything quite like this. He joined two different tours, but the language being spoken was Italian, so he couldn't understand the guide at all.

The rooms were magnificent. He saw the Sistine Chapel with the second tour and peered up in amazement. At the same time, he carefully listened for anyone speaking Polish. It didn't happen. The words of his village priest came back to him. "Don't do anything foolish. God will protect you." He could hear Father Niemuk's words as clearly as if the priest were standing next to him. Wally came to realize that defecting to the Vatican was not the answer. He would have to continue to bide his time.

Wally returned to the barracks and spent his last night ever in Rome. He arose early and took the bus to the train station. After an hour wait, a train heading north to the German border was announced. The trip north was at a much faster pace than his trip south. After a few hours, he was at another station past the border. He exited his train.

There was an increasing resolve to desert, but Wally had become more thoughtful and knew that he needed a good plan not to be caught and then shot.

That night, he returned to his base and went to bed. There were new ideas floating around that 20-year-old brain. He had to find a safe way to get away from this life. But within days, there would be new orders directing Wally to a new area field of conflict and another new country.

The Pieszka house in Poland.

The Chybie railway station that was used
so frequently by the Pieszka family.

All photographs provided by Wally Pieszka, except where noted.

Painting crew at Auschwitz, 1941. Wally is on the extreme left.

Auschwitz Camp 1. These are the buildings Wally painted,
including the wall sometimes used by firing squads.

Pvt. Wladyslaw Pieszka in his German uniform, June 1942.

German infantry marching through the Ukraine to Stalingrad, July 1942.
Wally is the second from the right.
Photo courtesy of German Federal Archives, Deutsches Bundesarchiv.

Andrew Kadzielnik and his brother
Wally Pieszka in Scotland.

Cpl. Wladyslaw Pieszka in his Polish Free Forces uniform,
in Scotland, September 1943.

Coal miners at Lochore, Scotland. Wally is fourth from the left.

Painting crew at Oxford, England, 1955. Wally is in the center.

Wally coming over on the *Italia* in 1956. Mrs. Pregnitz is behind him.

Wally Pieszka going through immigration in New York City, June 1956.

This is the letter from Bishop Julisea Bienku in Poland in 1958, assuring Wally's parish priest in Chicago that he had been baptized and had his first communion in the Catholic church. It allowed Wally to get married in the Catholic church in Chicago.

Wally and Mary's wedding at St. Anthony's
Catholic Church in Chicago, May 31, 1958.

Citizenship certificate, including his name change
from Wladyslaw to Walter, in February 1962.

Wally and
his mother, Sophia,
when he made
his first visit
back to Poland
in 1963.

Funeral procession for Wally's father,
Franciszeka Pieszka, in Poland, 1968.

Second trip to Poland,1978 at Auschwitz.
Emil, Wally, and niece Basha.

Wally and Mary at a family party.

Return to Poland, 1994. Brothers Frank, Emil, Andrew and Wally.

The Kadzielniks in Ilownica: Marcin, Karina, Ania, Zosia and
Janek (John), September 27, 2015, in front of the
home that was rebuilt so often on the original site.

Wally Pieszka and author J. Dennis Marek in Bonfield, 2017.
Photo by Cathy Marek

CHAPTER 20

LEAVING FRANCE

Wally's easier life in Italy and Germany came to a close. He had risen to lance corporal and was decorated for his service and wounding in Stalingrad. Now there was talk that sometime in the near future the English and Americans would try a landing in France or Belgium.

It was the summer of 1943. Clearly the war was not going as well as Hitler had planned. He had lost in Russia and North Africa. Sicily was invaded by U.S. Gen. George Patton and the British. There were occasional radio broadcasts in German. From what Wally could understand, there was no mention of reversals in the Russian Front. Some men mentioned that no use of the word success meant that there were losses. Wally couldn't really understand how a leader could say something that was untrue and later, when Hitler said nothing, it was interpreted that Germany was losing the war.

Wally's injured trigger finger was healing but deformed. He hoped his days as a fighting soldier might be over, but then Germany was drafting more and more old men and young boys. While his injury might keep him out of a prominent unit, he knew that he was still cannon fodder. He wouldn't be given a medical discharge.

Suddenly in the summer of 1943, Wally's unit was ordered to leave its home base and begin a move to northern France. The unit packed up its tents and camping gear. They were told that there would be no permanent housing where they were going. Wally was now attached to a Lancer Regiment, so that meant infantry.

About 200 men were being transported to somewhere in northern France. They traveled by train and then truck. The trip took no more than two days and they were dumped in an open field near a small French town.

Wally never knew exactly where they were. He was not privy to any orders and he had no map. His movement in France over the next few weeks was through a series of small towns and villages with names he could not pronounce. Each time it was with their tents and gear with a mess truck accompanying them. The food was decent. It was now midsummer, and the temperatures were warm and comfortable.

When his unit first arrived in France, it was clear that they were near the sea, whether they were near Normandy or farther east was just not known. The days were spent in shooting drills, exercise and some informational meetings for the officers. The group makeup was almost all German and Polish troops, but their uniforms were identical. The French people were respectful and obviously afraid of the German troops. Wally had minimal contact with local citizens and did not go into their villages.

The summer was passing. Some of the more experienced men talked of a possible invasion and the bloody consequences that would certainly occur. In spite of the safer conditions, Wally wanted no more confrontation with an enemy he neither knew nor disliked. He hated where he was, but there were no options. Thoughts of desertion often occurred to him, but like the time near the Vatican, language and his naïveté would greatly hinder any such attempt.

Things were not as bleak as Stalingrad. He didn't have that feeling of not caring whether he lived or died. He was no longer freezing to death or starving. His weight was back to normal. The shock therapy in Germany, whether needed or not, certainly hadn't hurt him. He had few dreams and no nightmares. He had come to a point where it might be better to just wait and see what happened next.

As so many times in Wally's life, fate, the grace of God or an opportunity seized would rule once again.

The answer to his future appeared in the form of a fellow Pole, now a German staff sergeant in his unit. Wally knew him only as Zigmund, with a last name of perhaps Kinofski. From his accent, Wally knew he was a Pole and soon learned that he had been a very high ranking officer in the Polish army before its defeat by the Germans. Unlike Wally's brother, Emil, Zigmund was brought into the German army and eventually was made a non-commissioned officer.

While Wally did not often engage in conversation with them, the other soldiers would often carry on lengthy exchanges. One morning, he heard Zigmund speak French to a local man, and later the same day he heard this same man speak English. Zigmund was clearly an educated man who was confident in his actions.

From listening to his German, Wally had no doubt that Zigmund's principal language was Polish. He could tell that Zigmund listened carefully to Wally when he did speak. It was clear that Zigmund figured out that Wally was, indeed, another Polish man who had been forced into the German army.

One morning in early September, 1943, he accompanied Zigmund on an exercise.

Risking all, Zigmund quietly said to Wally in Polish, "Would you like to see England someday?"

Wally did not reply. He had never thought of seeing England.

"Do you see those men over there?" Wally responded that he did.

"They are the French underground, the Resistance," Zigmund said. "I know them and have spoken with them. Be here tonight if you would like to see England."

Wally sensed a plan in the making, but he was unsure of exactly what Zigmund meant. Was it a trap to see which soldiers were loyal? Was it a chance to escape this death trap itself?

The man was quite brave to speak to him in Polish. He also didn't seem to have any fear of the Frenchmen he said were the underground, or that he wanted them arrested. The day took forever to pass.

As darkness started to fall, Wally obtained a pass to leave the quarters and meet Zigmund on what was an evening walkabout. No Zigmund. He looked around carefully for any sign of a trap, but the soldiers he saw were minding their own business and did not seem to pay any attention to him. There were no security forces present.

Then Zigmund appeared with another soldier. It was now quite dark. They started off together.

"We turn here," said Zigmund, as the three of them progressed down a village street. Wally had never been this far from camp in the three months he had been in France. He soon realized that they were headed toward the water. It appeared to be an ocean. Wally had no idea what was going to happen. He was just tired of war and tired of wearing a German uniform. He was willing to take this chance.

Some other men fell in beside them, all wearing German uniforms. As they approached the water, a large fishing boat could be seen a hundred meters from the beach. Some were already making their way to the boat by hauling themselves through the water with the help of several long ropes that were extended from the boat to the beach. The men were then climbing into the boat. Zigmund waited his turn and grabbed a rope, walking chest deep through the water to the boat. Wally followed suit. The water was cold but bearable. Other men continued to line up behind Wally.

Wally still could not shake the feeling that it was a trap or that they would be discovered. Inside his head, the two possibilities continued to churn. Could he go through with this and take the risk of capture and certain death? Could he somehow get back to his unit without discovery? If so, would the men here try to stop him from going back?

His stomach turned as he recognized that life as it was did not hold any safety either. He could be shipped out again. He could be sent to Yugoslavia and fight the partisans, or back to the retreating Russian Front. He could have to stay here and face an invasion from England. There were sure to be many more bloody battles.

The future was grim. It made no difference. His life was threatened either way.

Wally waded toward the boat. Was he preferring the unknown to the reality of his present position?

It took Wally several minutes to navigate the water, the waves and the cold, but the rope was a godsend. As he reached the boat and tried to get in, he lost his balance and completely submerged himself in the sea.

Now he was totally soaked. Hands reached out and with the sailors' aid, he was lifted into the boat. The fear that it was some kind of German trap soon faded from Wally's mind. All these men were doing the same thing: boarding a boat and, perhaps, leaving France.

When all the men from the beach were aboard, the corporal announced that the boat was sailing that night for a remote landing area in England.

The men were all Polish. The corporal stressed that they had to remain undetected by the German patrol boats. They would appear to be just French fishermen. Wally suddenly realized that this was the English Channel, these sailors were French and with their help, all these men were deserting the German Army by sailing to England -- the land of the former enemy.

Wally was still scared, first of being detected by a German patrol, second by starting yet another chapter of his life, and finally by the fact that he was freezing.

The men, now numbering perhaps as many as a dozen, hid under the sails, netting and equipment. With so many, it was impossible to hide everyone and fool a patrol boat from any appreciable distance. Wally took his chances on the deck, exposed to the night air and potential danger.

The sailors plied their trade with some nets so that it would appear that they were just another fishing boat trying to feed a hungry country. The night slipped into morning as they sailed. After a while, the pretense of fishing stopped. At this distance from shore, they were clearly not fishermen. Now only luck would keep them safe from a German patrol boat.

The hours passed slowly. Eventually the sun started to warm Wally and dry his saturated uniform. He didn't dare take any of it off, as the night had been quite cold and the breeze continued throughout the trip.

There was just a small ration of food that was shared by the soldiers. No one tried to take more than a meager amount. These men were now bound by a new association. They were a band of deserters who never wanted to join the German army in the first place. Now they all faced a new unknown. Would they make it to England? How would they be treated? What was their future? They had recently been the enemy, albeit reluctantly, of the very place they were going.

Then one of the soldiers spotted land. As the mainland of England grew closer, it was clear that they were not entering a major city or port as the area ahead was lined with trees. As they approached, they saw a small wooden dock extending into the water. The fishing boat, with the use of its motor, pulled in next to the dock.

"Go ahead. You are in England and safe. Soon you will be given clothing and food. There are trucks on the way," one of the sailors said in poor but understandable Polish.

Obviously, this group had done such a trip before. Wally exited and got into one of three or four trucks. Zigmund was not in his truck. In fact, Wally would never see him again.

There went another man who had contributed to Wally's survival, but again he was gone from his life.

Soon, they unloaded into a camp and were spoken to in good understandable Polish to unload and step into the tent. Once inside the tent they were told that they had two choices. First, they could be considered a Prisoner Of War and sent to a camp for the duration. As a POW, they would be treated well.

The second option was more demanding. Would they be willing to join the Polish Free Forces, be shipped to a Polish army camp and serve the Allies? They were told that the ultimate goal was to free Poland from the Germans and allow them to return home to their families.

No one chose to be a POW.

Wally found this a bit amazing. It would have been so easy just to quit, surrender, be fed and wait out the war in safety. They would be safe whether Germany or the Allies won. If it was Germany, they were captured soldiers. If it was the Allies, they were POWs.

In his case, Wally was young and virile, war-hardened and angry because he had faced the hardships and dangers of Germany's war. He had up until now only worried about himself and his own survival through this ordeal. Was he ready to strike back? Were all of these other men equally as ready to face the enemy who had once trained them? Would they really retrain to fight a German force, or would they merely exist to do the absolute minimum, so as not be forced into a POW camp? Time would tell as it appeared that all these men would be leaving the camp together.

Later, as he thought about it, Wally came to understand that each of these soldiers had been given the same no-choice proposition when being drafted into the German army. It seemed that they were all willing to turn the tables and now fight the very army that made their lives so miserable. Surely they all wanted to return home to their families in Poland at some point. What other way was there than fighting for that chance?

Sure, he could wait it out. But for once, Wally was in control of a decision. He made the choice. He wanted retribution. It now burned in him.

Wally did not hesitate in trading his wet German uniform for one of the Allied Forces. He was about to wear the second military uniform of his young life.

There was a short half-hour truck ride to a camp. Warm showers followed and new uniforms were issued. Clearly the uniform was the same as the British with added insignia indicating the wearer was in the Polish branch of the army. Wally had never seen anything like it, as he had only confronted Soviet forces. Only later would he find out that the insignia had been carefully designed just for Poles willing to fight the Germans.

One of the British soldiers asked for Wally's campaign medals, one for being wounded and one for serving on the Stalingrad siege. He reluctantly gave them away. German uniforms were done. While he would regret the loss of these historic objects later in life, he found relief in not being burdened with anything German.

Wally was taken to a smaller tent and instructed to sit down. A Polish-speaking officer, with his rank on his shoulder, started speaking. Wally could tell that this man was from southern Poland, just as he was.

"We are going to give you a new name. If you are sent to fight the Germans and, God forbid, are captured, you can't appear to be a deserter. If you are, they will shoot you. But if you appear to be another Pole fighting for his homeland, you might well be interned as a POW. Let's get you a name and some new papers," said the officer.

They decided on the last name of Holexa for Wally. He would be from eastern Poland, miles from his true home. He was allowed to keep a modification of Wladyslaw for his first name, so he would be able to react normally to that part of his past. The name change would also protect his family back in Poland. If he were to be arrested as a deserter, they might seek revenge and go after his family as well. There would be no letter home explaining what he had done or where he was. Wally's last letter home had been mailed in August of 1943. Wally's parents had no idea of their youngest son's current status nor even that his plan had changed.

Wally's family was notified by the German army later that autumn that Wally was "ver mitzed" or that he "got lost." In France, a number of German soldiers just disappeared. Some escaped, like Wally, but others were killed by the French resistance and their bodies hidden. Wally's family would not know whether he was alive or dead for two more years.

Wally had escaped being shipped to Yugoslavia because of his accident with the saw, and now the chance encounter with Zigmund had allowed his escape to England.

Wally never looked at his actions as desertion. One can't desert something he never chose to do it in the first place. He was proud to finally make his own decision regarding his future. So far, his life had been chosen for him.

CHAPTER 21

OFF TO SCOTLAND

The camp in England had no name. It was a transition station for men who had either "deserted" the German army, escaped as French volunteers or had been captured and had chosen to fight for the Allies rather than languish in a POW camp.

The barracks were simple but the food was plentiful. Wally found a bunk, stowed his new gear and went in search of the mess hall. As he sat to eat with the other men, several languages were being spoken, but most of what he heard was either French or Polish. He didn't recognize any of the men from the boat trip across the Channel, but he did speak Polish to several of them. One of the men told a joke in Polish and those who understood that language roared with laughter. Wally could not remember the last time he heard or at least understood a joke being told, but he joined the laughter. It felt good.

None of the Polish men discussed anything of importance. Perhaps they all feared that there was still some trick or ruse involved with all this. Was this truly even England? Wally didn't know for sure nor did he have a clue what England was supposed to look like. So he kept his conversation very simple and just observed.

There was discussion by those who seemed to be in charge. They spoke of the men taking a train and of a place called Scotland. Wally heard that word sometime in school, but it had little meaning to him. There was also talk that the men would meet other troops who were already training in a camp in Scotland. This camp was not called by a specific name, but by a word foreign to Wally. It sounded like Galacias.

On the third day, there was commotion outside the tent. The new recruits had been hanging around their barracks waiting for someone to tell them what was next on their agenda. They were speaking Polish, so Wally could understand for once and heard mention of a train. Soon, a captain entered the barracks and called for attention.

"You are now all soldiers of the Free Polish Army. You are in the Ninth Lancer Regiment. This afternoon you will be transported by train to Scotland, to a base near the city of Galashiels. There you will be assigned to new units and trained in various specialties. Some will be in the infantry, some in armor. Some may become paratroopers. That will be decided when you arrive. So pack up your gear and be ready to head out within the hour."

Wally packed his new uniforms and shoes. His knapsack was stenciled with the name "Holexa." He would have to get used to that, but at least his first name was still Wladyslaw, Wally to his new friends. The men were assembled and loaded in trucks.

After a short trip, they arrived at a railroad station where a train sat on the tracks. About 200 men in new uniforms were then loaded onto the cars. The train was military and made up mostly by passenger cars with a few military flatcars loaded with various pieces of equipment.

As they loaded, it became clear that while many were Polish, there were quite a few French mixed in. It made communication difficult for those in charge, trying to give orders. Unlike his days struggling with German, these men were helpful in getting the message across with slow speaking and hand signals. What a difference.

Wally looked for Zigmund, the man who had saved him in Normandy, but to no avail. He knew no one so far. None seemed to have been on his boat. But this was not new to him. He hadn't seen anyone he had known since his friend died in his arms in Stalingrad.

Time would tell where he would be assigned. He had thoughts about being a paratrooper, as some of the men had alluded to a need for such men. Then again, he had only been in airplanes when he was wounded.

The soldiers arrived in Scotland early the next morning. The train had made only two stops, and they had been fed three meals enroute. Trucks met them at the station. It was a short ride to Wally's new base with no name that he'd ever learned.

The men were unloaded and fell into their assigned barracks. They would spend their first full day in Scotland looking over the base and settling in to their new surroundings. All seemed mixed in their feelings and enthusiasm. Some were excited to be away from the German army, while others were obviously tired of war regardless of the side they were on.

Over the next few weeks, Wally was chosen for an armor company of about 20 men. All were Polish including the officers. Language was no longer a problem on the base. However, English was the new challenge to him as the men spent some time in the surrounding village called Galashiels where Polish was obviously not spoken. German was difficult, but it did have some word similarities. English, with its Scottish brogue, was really different for a Polish-speaking young man.

So with a longing for home, a sense of boredom, and a bit of uselessness, he threw himself into his newest adventure -- tanks. He was feeling empowered after all the years of subservience.

Because of his earlier finger injury, he could not fire a rifle very well. That was probably why he had been chosen for the armor unit and not infantry. Training with tanks was more than a new job for Wally. It was exhilarating. Wally and his crew practiced how to drive, maneuver and fire this huge new piece of equipment. Wally had never driven a car, a tractor, nor even a motorbike before the war, so it was all totally new and exciting.

Often, the crew would leave the base and head for deserted dirt roads. As long as it wasn't too wet, the treads caused only minor damage to the surface of the various roadways. Driving a tank, he experienced freewheeling with few restrictions. Along these roads were quite primitive farm houses, usually single story and poorly constructed. In some ways, they reminded Wally of home. Farmers trying to eke out an existence. He even recalled images of German tanks parked on his family's potatoes.

Often, next to the houses were barns or "bairns," as the Scots would say, for their sheep and cows. All the farmers had cows for the milk and butter, and sheep for the wool and mutton. It was a time of war for these rural people as well. The war had been going on for more than four years for England and Scotland.

While Scotland was not a priority target of the German bombers and rockets, the war affected every facet of life in the British Isles, from food and common household needs, to peace of mind. The populous now lacked so much. While the area was relatively safe, these people were tired and depleted of extra assets. The war machine had to be put first.

Wally was promoted to driver of a tank. It was driven with handles rather than a steering wheel. The brakes were fairly non-existent; one slowed the tank with the throttle and lowered gears. His training as a German soldier had not included any driving skills, but he took control of the tank with authority.

His inexperience in motorized vehicles did not seem to bother Wally's commanding officer. Wally climbed aboard and was shown the mechanics of driving this behemoth. The first two attempts outside the base were without incident. Unfortunately, on the third training mission, as Wally came over a slight rise in the road, the road abruptly ended in a T intersection. Wally's speed, while not fast, was substantial. He attempted to gear down the tank, but mistakenly geared it up. Also, unfortunately, there was a farm house where the road should have continued.

In spite of his efforts to stop, Wally drove right into it. The front end of the tank stuck in the wall, caving it in. He held his breath and was horri-fied about what he had done. He was able to get the monster machine stopped about three feet into the residence. There in front of him were two women in the back kitchen looking at their missing front wall and a camou-flaged tank sitting part way into their living room. They just stared.

The tank was undamaged and the crew was able to extract it without help. They tried to express their apologies, but Polish words just did not come across. Later in camp, the crew explained to their captain what had happened and they were assured that the cottage would be repaired. Wally heard nothing else on the issue even though it was his fault. Later, he thought of what those women would have been thinking. An invasion? He felt sorry that he could not have done or said more to them.

The weeks and months went by quickly. He was feeling more confident with his tank crew. Some of the crews in the other companies were shipping out. Some were told that they were heading to Italy, while others to France. D-Day had just happened. Because of the secrecy, no one in the camp had a clue it was about to happen until the landing was completed.

Once they heard the news of the invasion of Europe by the Allies, the joy of the men was immediately apparent. They each saw different possibilities for their future, although these dreams varied. Some hoped to return home to Poland and defeat the Axis machine in their native country. Some wanted to wait out the war in this safe haven.

Wally knew he was only counting time until he would get home again, but then there was a call for volunteers for a special mission requiring paratroopers.

Wally was tired of waiting. He felt that Polish tank crews would not be sent to Poland, but to France. He wanted to fight to free his home.

Perhaps the extent of the experiences he was forced to endure finally angered him enough. The role of self-preservation he so often assumed was changing. He had suffered enough and he was now ready to really fight back. His drive to make things right was long overdue.

Wally talked to his captain and made his wishes known. New training started within a week. New uniforms were issued with different insignias and coloring.

Wally dreamed of marching through the streets of Warsaw or Krakow with young women throwing roses at the troops from their windows. He was going to liberate his homeland.

CHAPTER 22

SEEING ANDREW

Time in Scotland passed. The war dragged on. Rumors abounded about who was winning or losing, but without much certainty.

No call to combat was made on the Polish forces at this time. Wally's unit had not been used in the D-Day invasion. After hearing of the number of Allied casualties, most of the Polish soldiers were glad that they weren't involved, but Wally was bored and unsettled. He was prepared to do something to help free his homeland from German occupation.

He worried about his mother and father. Did they have any idea that he was alive? Or where he was? His parents being merely told that he was "ver misted" had assumed he had been killed in some action.

There was also profound loneliness. Sure, the other Polish soldiers were friendly. They could enjoy a common language and some customs, but Wally missed his family, his home town and his old friends. Other than the one furlough, Wally had not been home since May of 1942, more than two full years ago.

Word came that the Allies were pushing inward. Wally's group knew that some Polish forces had parachuted into France behind enemy lines. None of those had been from his base in Galashiels. It seemed that the war was going well for the Allies. Information was also coming down that the Russians were pushing hard from the east, moving through Czechoslovakia and parts of Poland. Wally knew enough about the Russians and their Soviet ways that he feared for Poland. He so wanted to fight to free his country from all foreign nations.

Wally heard from some of his fellow troops that a special division might parachute into Poland and harass the Germans as they withdrew. This is what Wally wanted more than anything. He had two parachute training jumps and was certified as "capable." Out of a hundred volunteers, only 30 were selected. Wally was on the list. His finger had healed well enough to accomplish any necessary task.

Then a rumor came down that a division of Polish soldiers being sent to Italy was coming through their area. They would arrive at the local train station in Galashiels, march to Wally's base and be housed there for a few days before being shipped out. Wally had been in Scotland for almost a year and a half. He wanted to do something like this, but not by going to Italy. Why Italy and not Poland, he wondered.

As all the Polish soldiers had been given a new name, Wally's friends all had names that were fictitious. Often times when they were called, the new last name was used. The men often didn't turn around or acknowledge. It took a while for Wally to adjust to his new last name as well. Wally, now Holexa, had made a close friend named Emil Kulas, also a Pole, in his tank company.

Emil approached Wally at breakfast and said, "There are Polish troops coming here today. They will arrive at the station in an hour. Let's go greet them. We may even know someone."

Wally was not interested. He wanted to finish his breakfast and relax. It was Saturday. But Emil persisted.

"Come on. It will be fun, and it is boring here." Finally, Wally agreed to make the trip.

They walked to the station and went into the station house which sat above the train tracks and the platforms. The troops were just starting to unload. Both Emil and Wally scanned the disembarking men.

For a moment, Wally's heart stopped. There by the post -- could it be?

"Emil. Emil. That is my brother, Andrew. I have not seen him in almost three years. I know that is him! We have to get to him before we lose him."

Emil said he would run and get two tickets to go on the platform while Wally would stay and watch where Andrew went so they wouldn't lose him. Wally was literally jumping up and down in his impatience. Three years. Out of all the Polish troops, here was Andrew.

What if he had persisted in not coming down to the station? Fate always seemed to play a role in Wally's life.

Emil returned with two tickets, and they ran to the proper platform. There was no security issue since the two were in uniform. No one stopped them. They presented their tickets and ran down the platform. Wally came to a stop right in front of his brother.

"Andrew?" he managed to say, his voice cracking.

"Wlady, is it you? How in the world did you get here? The Germans sent a letter to Mama saying only that you were missing."

They fell into each other's arms. There was so much to talk about, but first they both cried; tears of relief, longing for family and frustrations with a war that neither had asked for.

Emil and Wally followed the troops as they marched to the base. They were to be housed in a separate part of the base from Wally's company. Wally got permission to spend time that evening with Andrew. Emil stayed as well. They talked the entire night.

"I was finally able to sneak away from the Germans in France. We had a boat and came across the Channel about 14 months ago," Wally explained. "How about you? How on earth did you end up in Scotland?"

Andrew replied, "After you were drafted, I stayed with my wife for a while, still acting as though I had tuberculosis. Eventually, my luck ran out. We were living in the village near Ilownica in my wife's house when I got orders to present for a physical. They soon learned that I did not have TB, and I was drafted," Andrew explained. He said his training was minimal since he had already trained in the Polish army before the invasion, and he was almost immediately shipped to Normandy.

"We knew there was to be a major invasion. We just didn't know where. I was near Bastogne when we were overrun by a British army. We surrendered. As we were being transported, I said something to a fellow soldier in Polish." The British guard heard him.

"Are you Polish?" the private inquired. Andrew explained that several of the troops were Polish. An officer appeared and asked those men of Polish descent if they would rather fight against the Germans instead of spending the rest of the war in a POW camp.

"I said I would gladly fight for the Free Polish Forces and recapture my homeland," Andrew said.

What was the chance of such an encounter? How ironic that they both survived this far and made it to Scotland in such different ways.

Andrew had a new name as well. He was now Andrew Glitt. Andrew explained that his newly formed unit was going to be sent to Italy. The southern half of Italy was in Allied hands, and the Polish troops would help Allied forces push the Germans and the Italians further north.

Wally obtained a pass from his sergeant to stay with Andrew the next day. It was here that Wally hatched a plan that would keep Andrew with him and not in Italy. Sure, it might mean parachute drops, but they would be together. Wally pleaded with his commander to have his brother transferred to Wally's company. At the same time, Andrew requested to be transferred to Wally's unit.

"Brothers? You don't even have the same last name," said the commander of Wally's unit. Wally explained that his name wasn't Holexa, and Andrew's wasn't Glitt. "I know that, but I have your real names and they aren't the same either. Pieszka and Kadzielnik; not even close."

Wally patiently explained Andrew's father's death in World War I and their mother's remarriage to Mr. Pieszka. The commander pondered the situation for a few hours. But in the end, the commander finally approved the transfer, as did Andrew's commander. Andrew moved into Wally's barracks. They were together. The next day Andrew's company moved out by truck without him. The brothers were now a team.

Wally did have one secret that he had kept from Andrew in their talks. He would have to share that information soon.

CHAPTER 23

PARACHUTES, POISONING, AND PEACE

Andrew was safe. He felt considerable relief being with his brother and not heading out for combat in Italy. However, Wally had not shared all his information with his brother.

Wally had been ready for something, anything. When Wally's commander had made the announcement that they were taking more volunteers for a Polish paratrooper program, he was one of the first to volunteer. It was explained that they would be trained in making combat jumps along with some basic man-to-man combat moves. Andrew could now be included. Wally's training began a few weeks before Andrew's arrival and was almost complete. If he joined, Andrew could catch up.

"Andrew, I have something to share with you. I am going to be separated from this company shortly and have been training in parachuting. So far, we have been left inside our own units, but that will change. We will jump into Poland at some point and confront the German troops. How do you feel about that? Would you want to join us in this attempt to free Poland? I learned that there is more room for recruits and you could catch up on the training," Wally both confessed and pleaded.

Andrew was not thrilled. Perhaps it was his age. He had years of life experiences. He had lost to the Germans as a Polish soldier, had then been drafted into the German army, was captured by the Allies, changed his uniform three times already, and now was back to being a Polish soldier again. Andrew had already experienced gut-wrenching situations in only five years. Yes, he wanted a free Poland. He wanted to return to see his wife, his parents and his other brothers. But to parachute into one's country with no idea about the enemy, the location where they might be dropped or the chance of success, it was just too much for him. He felt his first duty was to survive and be a good husband and father.

He declined the invitation but was allowed to stay with his new unit. Wally was disappointed, but not surprised. Perhaps the difference between 21 and 30 was material in one's views of the future. The whole idea of the consideration of a wife versus no wife was paramount for Andrew. Wally was anxious to get back into a fight, this time for the right side. Wally and Andrew talked for hours. While Wally completed his further training, Andrew did basic maintenance jobs around the camp.

Talk spread that the move was imminent. In a week, the volunteers would be leaving. Wally and Andrew drew even closer. They ate together, walked together and played cards together. They could not get enough of each other. It was like old times, when Andrew was the older brother and Wally the rambunctious child. Now they were both men, and one was going to embark on a life-threatening mission.

One noon, while on maneuvers with his commando training team, they broke for lunch, eating merely canned rations. The canned meat was shared, with Wally getting the end slice of corned beef.

The age of that can was unknown. Wally devoured his slice.

Then it happened. It started with massive vomiting, then diarrhea, followed by headache and chills. Andrew helped carry Wally to the infirmary later that day. The nurse found a cot for Wally and went for a doctor.

Upon her return, a young English-speaking doctor accompanied her. He asked basic questions. Wally understood some of the conversation, but some of the medical part was unclear to him. He tried to say that he must have food poisoning. Clearly the doctor already concluded the same. The doctor ordered medicine to clean out his entire intestinal tract.

Wally was still having massive diarrhea and intestinal pain. The nurse prepared the solution and Wally drank it. Immediately he felt worse and could not control his bowels at all. Now there was blood in his stool -- massive amounts of blood. Wally fainted.

When Wally gained consciousness, he had never felt so bad in his life. His stomach was wracked with pain. He was losing blood from his rectum and in his vomit as well. He was scared.

Andrew was waiting outside. The doctor never explained that he had administered the wrong medicine, but it was obvious to the nurse who wouldn't look Andrew in the face. His brother was bleeding to death.

Finally, the doctor stated, "This man needs blood. We have to give him a transfusion. We need someone who will match his blood type."

Andrew did not qualify. A Scotsman who was assigned to the hospital was placed beside Wally on another cot. The plastic lines for the transfusion were placed between the two men and the transfer of the needed blood began. In all, Wally would obtain three units of blood over the next two days. Andrew stayed with Wally all day and night. Still, he did not improve. He could not get up from the bed. Andrew helped him urinate and after a while was able to feed Wally broth and simple foods.

Andrew leaned into Wally's ear after a week of this medical care.

"I know you wanted to be a part of the liberation of Poland, but your volunteers left yesterday. They wished you well last night and asked that I convey that to you when I saw you today. I don't know if that is a great disappointment, Wally, but it may have saved your life." Truer words were never spoken.

Within a month, word came back that the parachute jump did take place. The Polish troops were mistakenly dropped into active German lines and were massacred.

Once again, Wally had narrowly avoided death.

It took Wally several months to recover completely. His weight reminded him of his days in Stalingrad. He was emaciated. Andrew was there every day, feeding him, cleaning him up and encouraging him to improve. After a while, Wally's temperament improved. He wanted to eat and get strong. Andrew and Wally even joked that since the men giving the blood for the transfusions were all Scottish, Wally would become a lot better at managing his money. They both laughed.

In the spring of 1945, the brothers still had no combat assignment. They had freedom to move around Scotland. Tank training was over for Wally, as was paratroop practice. Life was safe and somewhat boring. The brothers spoke of what was to happen with Poland when the war ended. When would the Allies free their homeland?

They heard of a massive German retreat from France back into Germany. There had been a last gasp attempt by Hitler at what became known as the "Battle of the Bulge." Finally the Germans were in full retreat However, no orders to go to France, or Germany or Poland were coming. The Russians were pushing harder than the American and British allies to free countries such as Poland and Czechoslovakia. The biggest push by General Eisenhower was into Germany and north. Poland and Czechoslovakia were being left to the Russians.

Weeks passed without orders. Perhaps there was no single point where these remaining Polish troops could be inserted. Propaganda overwhelmed the British Isles. From Churchill and Roosevelt to Stalin in the east, the news was solely German defeat after defeat. Wally believed most of what was being said, but there was no real news of Poland and how badly it had been damaged by the advancing Soviet troops.

It was becoming clear that he and Andrew would not be needed in the coming battles.

Then the announcement was made. Germany had surrendered.

Poland was occupied now by Soviet troops. General Patton's request to push on and take Poland and Prague had fallen on deaf ears with Eisenhower. Patton, considered a great general but a wild man, had continually harped to the press that the Russians were not to be trusted. He suggested that the Allies just keep pushing, driving the Russians back home.

His ideas were ignored by his leaders. Worse than that, Patton's outbursts were found to be damaging to the relations among Stalin, Truman and Churchill. The Americans wanted and thought they needed Soviet help in the Pacific to defeat the Japanese. Field Marshall Montgomery, therefore, got the gas and Patton sat with his battalion of tanks on the border of Poland and Czechoslovakia without fuel to run his tanks.

It was over. Poland and Czechoslovakia were now "liberated" but totally under the Communist regime.

A few letters from Poland came after Wally and Andrew had both written to Wally's parents and Andrew's wife. It was the first time the Polish side of the family knew whether these two men were alive or dead. The return mail, however, was filled with more bad news. As the Germans withdrew from the Russian Front, the warring between the two troops went back and forth.

Unfortunately, Ilownica was in one of the areas of this continued tug of war. The small village was a site of major artillery exchanges between the Germans and the Russians three separate times.

In one of those exchanges, the Pieszka home was demolished. Mother and father had been evacuated from the area, but had moved back in and were now living in the basement of their destroyed home along with Emil's wife, their child and his mother's sister, Cashia. The rest of the house was gone. Rebuilding for any of the Polish survivors was out of the question. There was no money and there were no building supplies. There was now no electricity in the rural areas, only kerosene lamps.

Andrew's home in Kiczyce, two villages from Ilownica, had survived the battles. He had a place to go and had a family. He was offered free transportation by the Allies to his home.

Andrew informed the authorities that he would go home in spite of the political problems. Wally, on the other hand, sat in contemplation. On one hand, he missed his country, his village and his family. On the other hand, there was no place for him to live. His family home was reduced to a rudimentary basement measuring 16 by 16 feet. There would be few jobs and Wally had minimal training other than making war and painting walls.

He was now 22 years old and had seen more than most people do in a lifetime. But he was not prepared for civilian life.

Wally liked Scotland. The people were a bit reserved, but the girls were cute and jobs were becoming available.

After hours of conversation with Andrew and weighing his future, Wally made the final decision to stay. Andrew was still there until late May. He was discharged from active duty and was sent to Poland by boat and trains. His war was over.

Wally went to the train station when Andrew was leaving. Parting was so difficult. Here were two brothers who had survived six years of turmoil, separated from their family, from each other, one wounded and poisoned but somehow still alive. They knew that they would not be able to see each other for a long time.

As Andrew boarded the train for his return to Poland, Wally couldn't let go of his hand. He knew that this was what Andrew needed and wanted, but here was the last vestige of family once again sliding out of Wally's life.

The tears flowed, the goodbyes were spoken and then there was only the waving as Andrew's train pulled out of sight.

Here Wally was again, alive and finally well, but alone. It seemed at times that he was destined to be alone.

CHAPTER 24

DRIVING FOR MADAM

The war was now completely over, everywhere. People were still talking about the atom bomb and places like Hiroshima and Nagasaki, but those names meant nothing to Wally.

Wally continued to live in the Scottish barracks at no charge, but that had to change. He was officially discharged from the army in September 1945. Wally wrote home immediately after the armistice in Europe, but it had taken months for any mail to arrive from Poland.

Before Andrew left for home, Wally and his brother devised a code to relay to Wally how things were at home if the mail was being censored. If things were good, Andrew was to say that the bridge was rebuilt and strong. If things were not good, he was to write that the bridge over the river is out. Eventually, Andrew wrote that the bridge was out.

After Andrew's departure, Wally heard of a landscaping course he could take for free just outside of Edinburgh. As a farm boy, he knew a bit about growing things but nothing about landscaping, specialty planting and creating an aesthetic lawn. Studying would not provide any income, but he was getting some money from the British government for his service and he could live in the barracks for free. Generally, he chose not to spend very much. Now that the war was over, he was sending what he could to his family in Poland. Thinking about becoming a businessman, Wally thought that perhaps the Soviets would leave Poland someday, and he could return to open his own greenhouse.

After starting the landscaping course, he learned that he could get a job on the rather large farm of a Mr. Lowe. Upon completing the landscaping course, Wally took a chance and wrote to Mr. Lowe of his certificate in landscaping, asking if he had a job along those lines.

He soon met this man who owned the farm. Mr. Lowe made a handsome proposal, "Wally, how would you like a day job of being a chauffeur for my wife? I would pay you a wage and give you a place to stay on the farm. It would be even better than the farm work and easier on your back."

While Wally had never driven a car before the war, now he had driven not only cars, but motorbikes, trucks and even tanks, and he could handle this job.

Wally realized that this was a real chance. Earn money and live in a place for free! How could it be better than that? He found out very soon.

Mrs. Lowe did not drive, so she needed to be driven places constantly: teas, luncheons with lady friends, weddings and shopping. When she left the house, Wally would often drop her at an arranged place and sit in the car waiting. Sometimes it was several hours, but he expected the job would be that way from a short conversation with Mr. Lowe at the very beginning. The Mrs. thought of herself as nobility because they were very rich. She also believed that the servant should wait with the car.

One afternoon after interminable waiting, Wally needed to use a washroom. He waited and waited, but could hold it no more. He locked the car and found a café with a urinal next door. Then he made a mistake. He went into the café and got a coffee in a paper cup. When he returned to the car, there was Mrs. Lowe staring at him and tapping her foot impatiently. She had been waiting! Probably no more than ten minutes, but waiting a lifetime, in her mind.

She scolded Wally without mercy, chastising him for going for coffee.

"You stupid Polack. Your job is to stay with the car, not go after coffee."

She then got in the door and refused to close it herself. Wally dutifully closed the door, got in the car and drove her home. He was angry. This was the dream job. He swallowed his anger and his pride, but he would not apologize.

Wally studied more landscaping when he could, but it seemed that Mrs. Lowe's need for the car and her driver took more and more time.

There was, however, a fringe benefit to come along. It seems one of the foremen at Lowe's farms was a man named Bill Ramsey. Conversations were fairly easy between Bill and Wally. At first, he instructed Wally in the operation of the farm and how it supplied much of the plantings and flowers that were being used to redesign lawns and gardens for the more wealthy Scots.

The war had been hard on the landscape. Not only were there bombs and fires, but fertilizer had been rationed. Chemicals often used to keep the plantings green were also part of the components used in many of the bombs and explosives. While water was plentiful, the manpower to maintain these gardens of the rich was woefully lacking from 1940 to 1945.

Wally and Bill struck up a friendship, and Wally was invited to the Ramsey home one Sunday afternoon. There he met Mrs. Ramsey and their two sons. More importantly, he met the Ramsey's daughter, Nancy, a beautiful and single young woman.

From the first time in meeting Nancy, Wally was smitten. Whenever he wasn't driving Mrs. Lowe or studying, he would head to the Ramsey house and court young Nancy. They went to movies and often went dancing. Wally was careful not to include a meal, as his funds were scarce and he was still sending money back to Poland with regularity.

The months passed and Wally was quite serious about Nancy. Her mother seemed to adore Wally, but the brothers were rather cool toward him. While father, Bill, had actually introduced the pair, it seemed that he wasn't all that pleased with the arrangement. It was obvious that religion was a problem. Wally still was a devout Catholic and the Ramseys were members of the Church of England.

While this was a certain hurdle for any relationship, it was not openly discussed between the couple. As the first year passed, Wally was quite serious about some kind of more formal step between the two. It seemed that men were in short supply after the war and women were much more plentiful. While Wally was a foreigner by birth and still spoke English with quite an accent, he felt an engagement and even marriage could work out with Nancy.

One spring night as the couple was coming home from a dance, Wally noticed that the Ramsey's front window was open as they approached the porch. Starting up the stairs, he heard Bill Ramsey's loud clear voice as he addressed his wife.

"This has gone on long enough. It is time we stepped in and ended this relationship. I will not have my daughter marrying a God Damned Polack."

Wally was crushed. He quickly and quietly said goodbye and returned to his quarters at the Lowe farm. That night, as he thought of Nancy, he remembered how close his family had been and how his parents had cared for Emil's wife for seven years as he sat in the POW camp.

He thought of the closeness Polish families had for each other, and that included in-laws. This relationship was not going to work. He knew it. That night he went to sleep with a heavy heart.

The job of driving Mrs. Lowe became more burdensome. She became more persnickety and demanding. Mr. Lowe was of no help. He knew his wife's ways and just stayed out of the fray. She was Wally's problem and Mr. Lowe enjoyed the time that she was gone with the car and her driver.

Wally was again waiting for Mrs. Lowe on High Street in Edinburgh. She had been gone for two hours and Wally was starving. He quickly slipped around the corner, grabbed an order of fish and chips from the local vendor and hurried back to the car. There she was, tapping her foot and "tsking" as only she could do.

Again she raised her voice. "Are you never going to learn? Why am I stuck with a dumb Polack like you?"

She ordered her door to be opened and instructed Wally to throw away the rest of his chips. He was told to start driving immediately.

That was the last straw. Two nights before, he had seen Nancy and the romance was clearly over, and now he was getting another tongue lashing.

He was about to just walk away from the car and quit, but common sense took over. He needed a ride back to the farm where he could pick up his clothes. The drive was fast and probably quite uncomfortable for the back seat passenger, but Wally didn't care. He slid to a stop in front of the manor house, opened the door, bowed and walked away, leaving the door ajar as well as Mrs. Lowe's mouth.

Wally threw his extra clothing in a basket and walked off the premises. He proceeded to find the employment office. He did not have the funds to start a landscaping business yet. He would have to save. He needed a good paying job for now.

CHAPTER 25

THE MARY COLLIER MINE

Had his temper cost him his livelihood? He decided that it hadn't. He had rights, too. With his small bag of clothing, he set out for Edinburgh.

He soon found a bed and board with a Mrs. Blair, a war widow who took in male boarders. She provided some meals. He learned that there were no Sunday meals, as Mrs. Blair would not cook on the Sabbath. Since he was still searching for a good job, he was there on Sundays and missed the two meals usually provided in Scottish rooming houses.

Wally had heard that the coal mines in Scotland were under-manned. All the mines needed able-bodied miners. Through an employment agency, Wally was directed to apply for a job at a mine named the Mary #1, but nicknamed the Mary Collier Mine, perhaps a play on words for a coal mine -- colliery. While Wally knew nothing of this name, most working class Scots and Brits were quite familiar with her.

The real Mary Collier had been a washerwoman in a small town near Sussex, England. She labored until she was 63. Although she was an uneducated woman, she had a talent for writing poetry. Her first poem was written in response to a poem written by a man named Stephen Duck. His poem, *The Thresher's Labour,* criticized working women, finding them rather useless. This untrained working woman wrote a poem in response that started to circulate. The question in the more educated world was how could such an uneducated woman respond with a poem of her own? Her poem, *The Woman's Labour,* spread through the country. It seemed as though the gentry feared a commoner who could write such poetry, while the laboring class had found a heroine.

The so-named Mary Collier mine was in Lochore, a ways from Edinburgh, but Wally was able to take a train, find the mine, apply for a job and find a place to stay with a woman named Mrs. Torschak. He had an attic room with its own outside entry. Mrs. Torschak's husband, Edwin, was also a miner at the Mary Collier and became a friend over the six years that Wally worked in the mines. They often walked together to work but not home. Wally would find out later why he always missed Mr. Torschak after work.

Wally's first few days were spent in a training program located at the entrance to the mine. He learned of the dangers of a mine. He was shown pieces of equipment and was told in brief how coal was mined below the very building in which they were sitting. He learned of the two elevators that ran deep into the heart of Scotland and how men went down, coal came up, and then men came up at the end of their shift.

Wally was not sure he liked leaving the open air atop the ground, but the pay was excellent, and he wanted to send home as much money as he could to help his parents rebuild.

There were two shifts. The late shift did the blasting and the first shift loaded the coal into "boogies." These small carts were used to fill conveyor belts with the coal for transport to the elevators. The later shift, in addition to doing the blasting, often constructed the support beams that kept the hollowed rooms from collapsing on the men removing the freed coal the next day. The first shift did the backbreaking removal of this fragmented coal.

On his first day of mining, Wally descended hundreds of feet into the dark hole. There were a few lights in the elevators. The beam on Wally's helmet often provided his only light.

When he first offloaded from the elevator, he noticed the smell. In some ways it reminded him of the battles in Russia because the cordite from the blasting had a similar odor to rifle fire. It brought back memories, most of which were unpleasant.

Wally followed several men through tunnels where the coal had been removed in the past. Lighting was minimal in these areas, as there was no longer any work being done there. These tunnels were merely passageways for the conveyors to transport the coal to the elevators from the new areas being mined. They walked around several conveyor belts as they went deeper into the mine.

Wally noticed openings with tunnels running into darkness. Sound echoed out of some of them from the workmen further in, while others were quiet and seemed abandoned. Some went lower as they branched off from the main tunnel, while others went upward. Wally had no idea why these tunnels were so constructed. It took all his concentration just to keep his footing.

After a few minutes walk, Wally went into an open area that was like a large room. The walls were black, and there were mounds of coal on the ground near carts. In the center was another conveyor. Several men shoveled the coal onto the conveyor, or if it was too far from the belt, they used the cart he had seen by the elevators. They shoveled the more distant piles of coal into the cart and pushed the cart to a conveyor. This was going to be Wally's job for the next few years.

Wally was handed a shovel and shown where to begin. The men beside him worked hard, but were careful to pace themselves. The shift was eight hours with few breaks, one being to eat a lunch that each man brought with him. Wally had no prior knowledge and spent that first lunch break with only the water provided in a large jug.

The men he first met that day were Scots, but Wally later learned that there were other Polish men working in other areas of the mine. Wally stayed fairly quiet, as there was no camaraderie as yet.

Around three that afternoon, the men almost in unison stopped shoveling. Somehow they knew it was the end of the shift. There were no bells or horns sounding. Wally wondered how these men all knew at the same time to quit working. He would later learn that all laborers have an uncanny sense of time, especially when a shift was over.

Wally followed behind his co-workers as they made their way to the elevator. Other men appeared from other openings. When they were all assembled at the elevator, some had to wait, as the first elevator was full and the second elevator was still descending from a previous load of coal being brought to the surface.

When he entered the second elevator, he stood against the back wall, feeling the vibrations as the cold steel cage rose. The ride took several minutes. As he left the elevator building, the sun nearly blinded him. It amazed him that he had spent eight hours in almost complete darkness. The reintroduction to light would continue to amaze Wally over the years. He never really got used to it. This struck him as proof that man was not supposed to spend so much time underground.

Wally followed the men to a building near the elevator shaft. They went inside. Along the walls were lockers and each man had one. There, the men stripped away the working clothes and carefully removed other sets of clothing. In the locker went the sweaty, grimy pants, trousers, jackets and socks, along with boots.

Wally had been issued work clothes at the start of the day and was given a locker. There were no locks on the lockers but the men seemed to trust each other. Once naked, the men headed to a separate room that was filled with toilets and sinks. Beyond that room were showers and towels. Almost all the men took time to slowly shower. It seemed their tired bodies gained energy from the warm flowing streams of water. Wally modestly joined them but was uncomfortable with his nakedness at first.

The first day was over. He smelled better and had kept his personal clothing clean. He walked to Mrs. Torschak's house. He did not see Mr. Torschak either in the locker room or on the streets. Wally later learned that Mr. Torschak never showered. He stayed dirty and just seemed not to care about his appearance. It was clear that Mrs. Torschak did not like this behavior, as Wally never saw them hug or kiss. Theirs was a strange relationship.

Wally quickly learned the work. It wasn't very complicated but it did require a great deal of effort every hour and every day. He was not as fit as he had been in the army. Driving the car for Mrs. Lowe and doing the odd jobs around the Lowe house and farm had not been very physical. Wally was exhausted at the end of each mining day.

While he had worked with other men in the past, they were under the direction of soldiers. Most times, he had worked under threat of punishment if he slacked during his stint in the two military forces. The same was true of his time in Auschwitz. People there watched how hard you worked. Here it was different.

Most of the men were at the same level of authority, namely the lowest. There was a foreman who looked in on each section of workmen periodically, but the men worked on their own. If the amount of coal loaded from time to time matched expectations, nothing was said. The men worked hard, but they did slack off a bit when the foreman was not watching. Wally learned that not all were going to give the company maximum effort each day. This was also new to him. Once again, Wally was seeing the working world in a different country with different needs for employment. In Poland, it had been for survival.

Over the months, nothing much changed. The pay was regular and fair. He loaded coal five days a week. He lived with Mrs. Torschak. Wally rarely went out on the town when he first arrived. Going out cost money, and Wally sent every extra pound back to Poland. There just wasn't much left.

Then one of the other Polish miners asked Wally if he was going to the dance Saturday night. His first instinct was to say no, but an interest was piqued. He asked how much it cost and was surprised to find it quite reasonable. The Polish man mentioned that there were always more women than men, another consequence of the war. Wally agreed to go. With this invitation, Wally began to cultivate a bit of a social life.

His weekends were spent at dances. Sometimes there were gatherings at a local pub and, on rare occasions, a group of miners and young girls from the town would head to Edinburgh for a day in the city. The young women were fun but chaste. Perhaps a stray kiss or hug but nothing more unless there was a serious relationship growing between couples. Wally had none of these relationships and was content to merely enjoy their company when away from his work in the mine.

The years passed. There was no special girl in his life. Wally's major social life was talking to Mrs. Torschak and receiving letters from home. He learned that communism was not a gift from above. His parents were under strict control. There was no way Wally could visit them. The regulations were endless, so he had to be satisfied with letters.

Generally, hard, physical work and rather meager pleasures do not make time pass quickly. In Wally's mind, however, this was just another time of survival. Life in Poland had been so demanding that his time in the coal mines was quite acceptable.

Wally was used to hard work with few or no rewards all his life. The family and survival were all that mattered. Now there were a few actual pleasures. He had a bed, a job, wages and a mission to help those at home. In what seemed a very short time, the years were passing by.

In the fourth year of his mining, his superior approached him.

"Wally, I want to talk with you after work today," said the boss one morning on his way to the elevator.

That was unusual. He wondered all day what this might be about. He was the hardest worker in the group. He said little and had no confrontations. The day seemed a bit longer than usual with this on his mind.

At quitting time, Wally showered, changed clothes and went into the office. He waited a few moments for the boss to finish what he was doing. He was asked to sit down.

"Wally, I have noticed how hard you work. We have a foreman who has been injured and will take some time off. I know your English is a bit rough, but I think you would make a good foreman. I would like you to take the job. There will be a pay increase with this position."

The boss looked at Wally, who did not answer right away. He wondered if he could handle a supervisory job. Would the men, mostly Scottish, respect him in his new position?

After a momentary silence, Wally answered that he would try this new position. The boss then explained what the job would entail and provided some hints on how to interact with the men with whom he had labored alongside but would now supervise. He went home that night with both excitement and apprehension. The new position would be interesting. A Polish foreman?

Since this was a Friday, Wally had the weekend to mull this change over. On Monday morning, he arrived at the mine a bit early, changed his clothes and noticed a posting on the company bulletin board that there were two new foremen, one being himself.

He went down the elevator as usual and was walking over to the loading area when he heard some grumbling. He heard words like Polack, a Polack foreman who wasn't Scottish. He even heard his name spoken. This was not going well.

Over the next month, production was down. While the blasting and structural work seemed to stay on the same pace, the loading of the coal, Wally's group's job, was not meeting expectations. The Scottish men were ignoring him.

Once, as he was just about to turn the corner into the room where the coal was being loaded onto a conveyor, he heard one man say, "That God Damned Polack. He shouldn't have the job. Freddie was in line, not some bloody Polack who can't even speak proper English."

There was more response from other men, none of it in Wally's defense. It was clear that the Scots were angry with the boss's selection of him as the new foreman. One miner even suggested beating Wally up as fair treatment, but there was no response to that statement. Wally was worried. While he really only hung out with Polish workers, he thought he was accepted by the Scottish miners as an equal. How wrong he had been.

In the next few days, the removal production went to an all-time low. He now knew that the slowdown was intentional. The men were going to make sure the new foreman was fired.

Wally wanted to talk to someone, but to whom? Maybe Mr. Torschak? Wally realized that he had no choice but to either face the problem or quit the job as foreman. He came home filthy. He ate his dinner and then drank himself to sleep.

After a few more days of poor production, Wally had his chance to talk about the problem. He was told to come to the office after his shift.

"Pieszka, this isn't working. Your crew is getting no work done and my boss is on me. What the devil is going on?"

Wally really didn't know how to respond. Should he tell of the jealousy the men felt? Should he come clean on what he believed was a deliberate slowdown to get him fired? Wally's skills did not include any background in management or even any experience in how to respond to a situation such as this. He finally settled with a shrug of his shoulders.

"I am going to have to relieve you of being a foreman. We cannot have a drop in production. You will go back to your former position as a laborer." And with that, he dismissed Wally.

Wally did not know how to feel. In some ways, he knew he had let the boss down. He hadn't faced the crew and brought attention to the real source of the problem. Then again, he hadn't risked the miners being fired for intentionally slowing production. He hadn't done anything. Perhaps that was his role in life, one of no decisions.

As he pondered what he could or should have done, he came up with a plan. He would let it be known that he surrendered the position of foreman, in that he felt he was not capable of doing the job. That way, the men would not suspect he had said something that would threaten their livelihood. At the same time, he wasn't admitting that he was "fired." Perhaps for the first time he worked out a plan that would suit himself best and not someone else.

That evening, as he walked home from the mine, he noticed a woman sobbing on the steps of the Catholic church in the village. Wally approached and tried to comfort her the best he could. Slowly, she explained that she was crying for her five sons who had died during the war. Three had been taken to an "orphanage" by the Russians and just disappeared. Two were taken away in cattle cars, probably for the mines in

Siberia, but were never to be seen again.

Wally learned that her name was Mrs. Zalas and her husband also worked in the mine. He helped the lady up and walked her to her home. Wally later met Mr. Zalas at the mines and the three became friends, sharing stories of Poland and the way things were before the war in their homeland. It was good to revisit his home with people who knew the old Poland, but the sadness of losing five sons hung heavy over both of the Zalases. This was the start of a friendship that would last for years.

The next morning, Wally carried out his plan and told the men that he was back as one of them, having surrendered his position as a foreman. They looked at him with surprise, but no one said a word. They all went back to work at their former pace. Soon, they found out that they had a new foreman, but it wasn't Freddie, the man they thought wanted. Wally found that interesting. Perhaps the men didn't know much about running a business, either. Their thoughts that Freddie was the man for the foreman's job were never to be tested.

Wally pondered all this from time to time. He was pleased with his approach. Perhaps some time in the future he would say what he really felt, regardless of whether some fellow workers didn't like it.

Life went on. Wally continued to shovel coal, dance on the weekends and every two weeks send money back to Poland. The animosity toward Wally disappeared. In spite of the friendlier co-workers, Wally was thinking if he couldn't be a foreman, where was life leading him now?

Then, a few weeks after being relieved of that duty, another disaster occurred. Once again, Wally faced a deadly event that would alter his life.

Wally and his crew were working in a shaft that ran upward from the elevators. The conveyors lowered the coal down to the large room where the two elevators were located. The day started as every other day. The workers arrived, walked through empty rooms where the coal had been removed and into the shaft that had been the scene of blasting the evening before. Coal was on the ground and the crew began their tedious task of getting the coal to a conveyor which then made its trip down to the elevator room.

"Flood! Flood!"

The alarms echoed down the tunnels while shouting rang through the shaft where Wally and his crew were shoveling. At first, Wally had no idea what this meant, but the others did.

"We have to get to the elevators and get out of here!" yelled one of the men. The entire crew started running toward the elevators and Wally followed. About 100 yards from the elevator room, they encountered five or six feet of water, and it was rising quickly.

Wally had never been told that there were underground springs near layers of coal. Generally, the blasting had no effect on these underground streams and they stayed contained. Sometimes, concrete was poured to seal potential leaks of these springs.

Somehow, the blasting the night before had weakened the stone and coal that held back such water. A break in the wall had released a roaring flood of ice cold water.

Wally didn't swim well, but he felt he could stay afloat as he saw the miners enter the freezing, neck-deep water. He followed as they went deeper into the elevator room. The room itself was only nine feet high, and there was no more than three feet of air at the top.

Wally could see the one elevator was there and a few men were inside. Whoever was running it had not let it go all the way to the floor, as it then would have been completely under water. The door was open, but it would not have held back water anyway, as it was metal cage.

Wally floated and struggled along the ceiling of the room. He still had his boots on and they weighed him down, but he swam as best he could toward the open elevator door. If it left, would there be a chance of getting up with the other one?

He was not about to take that chance. He pushed his way ahead, passing some men who were moving slower in the freezing water. He helped one man next to him who kept going under the water. With his help, they finally reached the elevator and together floated inside.

Several more men entered and the elevator was now packed. Someone knew what to do, or someone was able to signal someone, and the elevator began to rise, leaving dozens of men behind. There had been no more room, anyway.

The ride up took more time than usual. Water spewed out of the cage as they rose. Wally was still freezing, but at least he was out of the water. The other men were silent. They knew how close a call they had just survived. One was praying, perhaps giving thanks, or perhaps praying for the men who were left behind. Surely the water would continue to rise until something was done to seal the break and the water was pumped out. But that could be days.

After what seemed a long time, the car arrived at the top. Some workers and medical personnel awaited them. Some of the men had cuts and bruises, but most were just terrified and wet.

Wally was scared but uninjured. He headed for the showers and some warmth. As he stripped off his soaking wet clothes, he looked at his locker and then threw the clothes on the floor. He was done. He was not going back down into that mine or any other mine.

He had survived his work at a death camp, Stalingrad, a serious wound, strafing of his hospital tent, shock therapy, a one-way trip to Yugoslavia, an escape from the German army, missed being air-dropped back into Germany, being poisoned by his own doctors, and now this.

As he went to sleep that night, he prayed for guidance. Mrs. Torschak had been terrific. Her husband had survived as well, and perhaps was clean for the first time in years. Her supper was hot and wonderful, but Wally had a great deal on his mind.

There was talk about how many miners might have died that day, and how it was the mine company's fault. But this was not the principal thought running through this ex-miner's mind. What was next in the saga of Wally the survivor?

While flooding of mine shafts was apparently not that unusual, it shocked Wally. In spite of all his prior close encounters with danger and potential death, he wanted no part of the depths of Scotland any more. He would work on the surface in the future.

The cleanout and pumping of the mine took weeks. All the miners were laid off, and a different crew of men arrived to rehabilitate the flooded mine. The miners lounged and went to movies, but they received only a small compensation as they waited for huge pumps to be loaded into the shaft. Eventually, the water was removed. The offending stream was emptied and then sealed off. One of the men who did get to work on this repair was Mr. Torschak.

Wally told no one of his decision to quit. He was able to collect enough to pay Mrs. Torschak for his room and board. He did not tell her of his impending decision while he pondered a new profession.

There was a daily newspaper by the name of *Jednich* published in Edinburgh that was written in Polish. Copies arrived in Lochore only a day late. Wally pondered possible employment opportunities for a former soldier, miner and car driver. The only special skill he had was his painting background. He read want ads looking for something he could do.

After ten days of searching, Wally was once again rewarded for his diligence. There it was, an ad seeking painters. The only problem was that it was far away, in Oxford, England. There was an address and Wally wrote immediately in the best English he could. He couldn't ask for help from people who did not know his desire to depart this area and profession, at least not until the compensation from the idle mine stopped.

Wally described his prior experience. He wrote of his training, but downplayed the fact that he was not allowed to become a full tradesman in Poland under the German occupation. He stretched the truth a bit. Just before he mailed the inquiry, he found a friend who he could trust and who spoke good English. With some trepidation, Wally shared his letter, had it edited and sent the rewritten copy to the employer in Oxford. Oddly, he received a reply, but from a London address. It seems that the headquarters was in London, but there was a large reconstruction project under their control just outside Oxford. They were looking for painters for this new project.

The letter indicated the terms of employment and a start date. It was a long trip from Lochore to Oxford, a return trip for belongings was not likely. That evening, he shared his news with Mrs. Torschak. She said that she was glad for him, but would miss him and his company. They had become somewhat close over the years. Her husband gave her no companionship, so her renter had become her friend and to some extent, her confidant. It was painful for both, but they knew it had to be.

Wally explained his desire to never again go below ground. While the death toll was relatively low, the frightening experience in the mine would stay with Wally for years. He had thoughts not unlike those in Germany after Stalingrad before he received his shock therapy. While he knew much of the therapy was a gift from the Polish nurses, over time he came to realize that it had done him some good. This time, however, he would have to work his way through it by himself.

He was leaving the few friends he had. Once again, he was alone.

He went to the mine office and explained that he was not coming back. He was not alone in this decision. Several miners handed in their equipment already. He received one last pay check, and with a somewhat friendly goodbye, he was off. He squared his account with Mrs. Torschak and made his way, with all his belongings, to the train station. They consisted of one suitcase, a rolled-up parcel of extra coats and shoes and a small package with his papers.

The time between the flood and his departure was only about three weeks, so there was not much loss of income. The bi-weekly sending of money back to his parents, however, had to stop for a while.

Once again, Wally was on the move, and once again, he was in search of lodging and a new life.

While he traveled, Wally had thoughts about a possible return to Poland. With the Communists in control, however, it was almost impossible to visit. For now, there was no way he was going to move back permanently. Andrew's coded messages from his family carefully shared the dire conditions in Ilownica. The reconstruction had taken forever. Jobs were available at pitiful wages as the inefficient socialist state was in full force. Without his money, the family wouldn't have been able to rebuild the family home as much as they had. If he moved back, there would be no outside income. He had to stay away, be it England or Scotland.

CHAPTER 26

THE PAINTING BUSINESS

The train ride did not take as long as he had anticipated. While Wally had ridden trains to Edinburgh, he hadn't been this far away from the coal mining town for a long time. He rather enjoyed the trip and the excitement of starting fresh. He realized that he had grown tired of mining, but it took the flood to move him to thinking of his future again.

Perhaps Wally only moved as a result of a calamity. His farm life ended with a stab at painting when the Germans invaded. This ended when his teacher was drafted and he was forced to go to Auschwitz, only to be forcibly drafted. His wounding sent him out of Russia. Perhaps his desertion was his own choice, but to join the Polish Free Forces was an act of free will over being a POW for years.

As he readied for his first day in his newest occupation, he thought about Mrs. Torschak. He would miss her, but she had gotten on his nerves in the last few months. She had been constantly encouraging Wally to date her daughter, Maggie. He felt bad that he had not followed up on the hints, but Maggie just did not excite him. Perhaps leaving was good for another reason. He seemed to be going nowhere with his life.

As the train arrived in Oxford, Wally heard there was a large and important university there, although education at that level was something he never pondered. He heard about English and Scottish students passing their "O levels" and then their "A levels" before going to the university. He didn't even have an O level education. Going back to school did not appear as a possibility, as he needed to work and have money. His Polish sixth-grade education did not make him ready for further English education.

His first view of Oxford was stunning. There were many old buildings that were undamaged, or at least had been repaired since the bombing just ten years prior. He took his suitcase and walked to a bus station, passing many historical and majestic buildings. He had seen nothing like this in his home country and just a few such buildings in Edinburgh.

His destination was Kidlington, a small town ten miles away. The bus ride was short and soon he was in a place that caught his interest. Kidlington was quaint. He knew small towns and villages from home so he found comfort in walking through a small town with its shops and winding streets.

He checked into a reasonably priced hotel and found a pub that served fish and chips. After eating a quick meal, he headed back to the hotel to await tomorrow's meeting with his new boss.

Wally arose early and skipped breakfast. He wanted to be early for his appointment in order to make a good impression. He found the office and entered. A man introduced himself and spoke to Wally in English. After a few questions, the man changed to Polish. Wally was thrilled. A Polish boss could make life a lot easier. There would be no language problems or anti-Polish prejudices.

The boss explained that there were 15 to 20 painters working under him. There was a large construction project for residential buildings, and they all needed to be painted. The boss further explained the pay scale, which depended on Wally's speed and ability. Wally was to be watched for a few days at the beginning to evaluate his skill level.

Wally was surprised by the informality. There was no request for his papers. He was to be accepted as an apprentice. While Wally had never risen to that level in Poland, his skill level had been fairly good, and he was able to lead the boss into believing that he had been an apprentice in Bielsko before being sent to Auschwitz. After a few more questions and only a couple of forms, Wally was free to look for living quarters and painting clothes.

The next morning, he started. His crew was painting the interiors of several single family houses. The work was easy. His physical strength was incredible after all those years of shoveling coal, and his stamina was unending. He worked at a pace faster than most and never seemed to tire.

After three days at the hotel, Wally found a boarding house. An ad in the local paper put him in touch with another widow who rented out part of her big house after losing her husband in the war. Frances Ramsey worked in a restaurant part-time. This allowed her to bring home extra food and unused portions of daily specials. She used this food to supplement supper for her boarders that evening. Generally, the food was good, but Wally soon tired of her goulash, made from a conglomeration of left-over meals at the restaurant.

There were two other male boarders in the Ramsey house, one a Ukrainian, the other a Polish man, but the Pole was from an area near the Ukraine. Both were painters for the company. Generally, Ukrainians and Poles did not get along all that well, but Wally made an effort to co-exist. He liked Mrs. Ramsey and wanted to stay in spite of the food there.

Wally purchased sufficient painting clothing from a shop in the town. For the first time in his life, he was given credit at the shop since he was painting for one of the area's largest employers. At age 32, he now had more personal items and clothing than could fit in his one suitcase.

Since he had not been employed for a few weeks, he was a bit short. The credit was very useful.

After a week of painting, the boss called him aside. "Wally, you are doing a good job. You are showing up some of the other men with your effort. We will pay you at the highest apprentice rate."

Even though it had been 15 years since he painted in Bielsko, he hadn't forgotten much of what he had been taught so long ago. His pay was just as good as the coal mine, and the work was so much easier.

Time went on. Wally went to movies, dances on occasion and visited the odd pub on the weekends. There he learned to play darts. He found no women who attracted him, but life was good, and the people were easy to meet. He did wonder if he was bound to be single his entire life.

One of the pubs, the Dun Cow, had something of a strength machine. One put in a shilling and squeezed the handles. Depending on one's strength, shillings would be forced out of the machine. Generally, the player got nothing. Sometimes someone might get two or even four. At the end of the evening, the barkeep emptied the machine of any shillings that were left. Wally had to try.

He had come to the bar with a friend from the painting company, George Hans, and told George that he thought he could do well on this machine. George was a bit dubious, but he had no idea how strong Wally had become working in the mines.

With several men and women watching, Wally inserted his shilling and began to squeeze the handles. He just kept squeezing and shillings were raining out of the machine and into the tray below.

He counted his winnings. There were 35 shillings in the tray. This windfall happened a few times until all the patrons refused to follow Wally, as the machine was always empty. His reputation for strength was soon well known at pubs that had the strength machines.

After about 18 months, the company announced that the work was coming to an end in Kidlington. The projects were completed and the company was heading back to consolidate in London. At first, a few men were laid off, and it became obvious that soon there would be no work.

Wally's boss approached him at the end of a work day and told him that the company had room for him in their London operation. Would he like to move to London?

Wally contemplated such a move. He liked Kidlington and the people. While he liked the smaller size of the community, he needed to work. Fortunately, through his painting, Wally got to know many of the local people, including people who needed painters from time to time.

Wally turned down the offer to work in London. He had saved some money and decided it was time to start his own business. He thought back to the days in Ilownica when he envied the shopkeepers and small businessmen. He thought of his Jewish girlfriend and her father. It was time to try.

With some of his extra funds, Wally bought a used van. After some negotiations, he was able to buy the van for 150 pounds sterling. He knew how to drive in England on the left side of the road after his year of chauffeuring and driving the company truck to job sites. He met a glazer, George Kavanagh, who also worked for the company. George, an Irishman by birth, agreed to work for the Polish "boss," a first for Wally.

Wally was in charge of his own life now.

Wally outfitted the van with ladders, drop cloths, paints and brushes. Money was tight, but soon the demand for his little company was almost too much for two men. His debt was quickly reduced. Those who sold Wally equipment on credit were repaid. Money once more flowed to Poland.

George converted from a glazer to a painter over the months and was a real asset to the business. With his help, Wally painted both exteriors and interiors. The two men were working six days a week when the weather permitted. George Kavanagh became a good friend and companion for Wally's time in Kidlington. He was also the first full-time employee Wally ever had.

But then another chance for change entered Wally's life. One rainy weekend when the exterior painting had to stop, a Ukrainian friend suggested they take the train to London.

"Why do you want to go to London?" Wally asked.

"I am thinking of immigrating to Canada. I have been here since 1945. I want to see that other side of the Atlantic," his friend replied.

"But now we have to pay if we go to other countries. The deal of free passage to the United States or Canada is over," said Wally.

His friend replied, "So what? I have never made the kind of money I have been making here. I can afford it. So can you, Pieszka!"

That morning, they took the train to London and were there by 11 a.m. His friend had an address for the Canadian Consulate, and had been told that emigration could be done through an embassy or even a consulate. Wally tagged along, not really interested in making a move to another foreign country, but more for the trip and the companionship.

On the way to the Canadian Consulate, there in the middle of the block was a large building with a larger sign on the front lawn that read The United States Consulate.

The United States. Chicago. That is where Polish people go, not Canada.

"You go ahead. I am going in there. We can meet later," said Wally.

In retrospect, Wally could never explain this rather rash act on his part. He had wanted a business he could run. He finally had one. He owned equipment and even a vehicle. He had employees and could sit back a bit. Physical labor was certainly a necessity, but he had help.

Regardless, Wally Pieszka made another life-changing decision.

CHAPTER 27

ALL POLES GO
TO CHICAGO

Wally entered the American Consulate and found a receptionist at a front desk. She greeted him in an accent to which he was not accustomed. While he had been speaking English for 13 years, the accent was always British, Scottish, or Scottish with a Polish accent. She sounded unusual. Her speech was rather flat but easily understood. It was his first encounter with an American other than the occasional soldier who had stayed in Scotland after the war, but that was rare.

"Can I help you?" she asked. Wally was a bit tongue-tied. He knew what he wanted to ask but was not at all sure of what he wanted in the long run.

Finally he blurted out, "I might want to go to Chicago." And that started the process.

First she asked his name and then a question for which he had no answer. Did he have a sponsor? She then asked if he had been to the United States before. Was he a veteran of the war? Wally answered most of these easily, but the question about a sponsor puzzled him.

"All immigrants going to the United States must have a sponsor," she replied, after he said he didn't have such a person.

"There are many people in Chicago who will act as a sponsor, as it is a popular destination with many immigrants. But why Chicago?"

Wally took a moment to respond and replied, "All Poles go to Chicago."

The receptionist laughed and asked him to take a seat. She told him someone would be with him shortly. He took one of the chairs and waited. It didn't take long before a well-dressed man in a suit called out his name. Wally followed the man into an office.

"I understand that you want to go to America. I am assuming that you mean on a permanent basis. So we will have to fill out some forms in order to get you an entry visa." With that, the papers and the questioning commenced in earnest.

Wally soon confirmed that the free passage that he had heard about to help Allied veterans to immigrate to America, Canada, Australia or New Zealand had expired some years before. He was going to have to pay his own way and would have to book his own transportation.

The man explained that crossing by passenger ship was cheapest, and there were several ticket classes on a ship, from First Class to Tourist. He then helped with the information needed to obtain the visa, and added that he could even find Wally a sponsor. It seemed that the Polish Consulate had names of people willing to accept immigrants and act as the sponsor.

With the paperwork complete, the man explained that he should not try to book a ship before late July of that summer, 1956. Completing the application and getting notification of a sponsor would take some time. The man sent him to the Polish Consulate.

Wally went there immediately. They answered many of his questions. It was comfortable speaking Polish and the staff was able to help him obtain the proper English papers so that these could be used in obtaining the American travel papers.

They even suggested that they could secure a person in Chicago to act as his sponsor. He would be notified by mail directly from the sponsor. Wally thought that in spite of the Polish government now being under the control of the Communists, the helpfulness was sincere.

Wally left the Polish Consulate with a fistful of papers and a head that was spinning. What had he just done? Here he was with a business, a van, equipment and an employee. Now he was about to book a trip to move to a foreign country that he had never seen.

For some reason, it felt right!

He knew, after the freedom he had enjoyed since the war ended, going back to Poland was never going to happen. The conditions under the Communists were only slightly better than those before and during the war. Scotland and England had treated him well for 13 years, but his personal friends were few, and his roots in this country were not deep. Perhaps things would improve even more with a move.

Wally met his friend, as arranged, and the two of them stopped for a beer at a London pub before heading back to Kidlington. Both had determined looks and were quiet for a while. When they began to tell of their experiences that day, they quickly learned that their new information was quite similar, even though one was from an American Consulate and the other from a Canadian Consulate. Both were told that they would have to pay their own way, and both were asked the same questions about why they wanted to emigrate, and whether they had a sponsor. Wally had not been very informative on the question of his desire to go to Chicago, and that was probably because he really didn't know in his own heart.

Wally continued his painting business that spring as he waited to hear from the American government and from this American sponsor.

A letter from the sponsor came first. A woman named Francine Bobetska wrote him that she would act as his sponsor. She was of Polish descent and had a boarding house in Chicago. He was to stay there upon his arrival. The price of his room and board was noted, as was a rather strange request. Mrs. Bobetska clearly indicated in her letter that new arrivals were expected to bring their sponsor a present. She also stated what that present was to be. In this case, she wanted a full setting of English bone china and he was to bring it with him on his trip to America.

With this much in hand, Wally went to a travel specialist in Oxford to book passage for New York. Remembering what the man at the American Consulate said, Wally booked a ship leaving in late July of 1956. There was one big catch. This ship at the great price was leaving not from England but from Gibraltar. The specialist informed him that arrangements could be made for the travel to Gibraltar. The total cost would still be cheaper than from England if he wished to go Second Class. He bought the ticket.

Now all he had to do was sell his painting equipment after finishing two outstanding projects. The time flew by before the van and ladders were sold.

Then, he received a letter from the American Consulate confirming that he had a permit to leave for the United States as soon as he could arrange his transportation. This came so suddenly, Wally had to rethink his plans. He had promised delivery of his equipment for the first week of July, yet it was only late May.

Once again, Wally made a trip to the travel agent in Oxford. "Can I exchange my ticket from July to something earlier? I received my papers much sooner than expected," he explained.

The agent searched her records and announced, "We have a sister ship leaving June 12. I can make the ticket exchange without an extra charge. One thing, however, on this new ship, the *Italia,* you will go Tourist Class rather than Second Class. There is only one ticket left, but you can leave from Portsmouth, England. No need to travel to the continent. This ship is larger and there are more classes for travelers."

This last part meant nothing to Wally. The price was the really important issue. He had been hoarding his money carefully for the last few weeks, including the money from the sale of his business assets. To go without an up-charge was crucial. He agreed to change his ticket. He was to sail on the *Italia* in two weeks from Portsmouth, bound for New York City.

Wally next went shopping for china for the first time in his life. He knew nothing about such upper-class things, but at a store in Oxford, a gracious lady attended to him. She seemed rather surprised that this man wanted bone china, but Wally explained why he needed to buy something. They discussed pieces and sets, different brand names and quality, place settings, and platters, and finally tea services. After much debate, Wally purchased four settings of tea service plus a teapot, creamer, and sugar bowl.

All the delicate china was carefully wrapped for a sea voyage, and Wally returned to the village to await his departure. Time now seemed to go quickly. He explained his sudden change of plans to his landlady. She was gracious and told him there would be no additional charge for an early departure, since he had been a good boarder for two years.

He also wrote to his brother, Andrew, asking him to break the news to his parents. He did not have the courage to write his mother directly about not fulfilling her dream of having all her sons back in Poland.

Emil was a bricklayer in Ilownica and now had a grown son, Janek, who was living with him and Wally's parents, helping them as they grew older. Frank was still in Kiczyce, just up the road from Ilownica, and back in his profession of tool and die making. Andrew was nearby working as an engraver of gravestones. Wally knew his parents were in good hands.

The day of departure arrived. Wally packed his belongings and the tea service into two suitcases. He said goodbye to his good friend and employee, George, and took the train to London. There he transferred to a train for Portsmouth. He was told that he could board the ship that very night, which saved any lodging charges. The ship was to sail at 8 a.m. the next day.

As he sat in his compartment in the Plymouth train, he saw a Polish man he knew in Scotland but had lost track of since his move to Kidlington. Mr. and Mrs. Zalas, of all people, were also taking the *Italia* to New York. More than that, they were also going to Chicago.

Wally remembered meeting Mrs. Zalas in Lochore as she was sitting on the steps of the church crying over her five sons who died in the war. Now they were booked on the same boat to America. Wally had not seen the couple since leaving Lochore.

Wally arrived in Portsmouth, and said goodbye to the Zalases, as they were traveling a different class on the ship. He boarded a bus that took him to the dock. This ship was enormous. Wally noted that there were several gangplanks leading up to the main decks of the vessel and he was able to determine that some were for First Class and Second Class. The final one was marked Tourist Class. He took the latter.

Wally showed his ticket to the steward at the foot of the ramp and received instructions on where to go once on board. He climbed the gangplank with his own luggage. He could have had the steward deliver the two cases to his cabin, but he knew there would be a charge and a tip. He could carry his own.

His "cabin" was shared with a half-dozen other men, and they all shared a single toilet. Wally was already uncomfortable. He had been told that his trip on the other ship was to be spacious and comfortable in Second Class. Wally began to understand the divisions of classes in society and now on ships. He had certainly traded down. And the trip was to take ten days.

He selected a top bunk, threw his cases on it and went looking for the deck. His room had no direct access to a deck, nor did it have a porthole. He reached his sleeping room by walking down a long interior hallway. Wally needed fresh air and found the deck reserved for the Tourist Class. He found the dining salon for his class and was able to determine the times meals were served. There was to be an evening meal in one hour.

He ate his meal at a large table and kept to himself. He still had not become comfortable with his new surroundings, nor was he completely comfortable yet with his decision to leave all things known to him for a new place and a totally new life. He knew he had to begin making new friends.

After dinner, Wally walked to various decks surveying the enormous ship. He had seen warships on occasion and some in port when he came over the English Channel in 1943, but he had never been on a ship this size. It was mammoth. One could walk ten minutes in a given direction and not reach the front or back of the ship.

He knew the multiple decks were divided by class of ticket, but no one challenged him as he strolled, although he had been told that passengers with his ticket were restricted to the Tourist deck.

Wally returned to his cabin when it was dark. There were men sitting around in the large room playing cards and other games, but he was exhausted. He met one of his cabin mates, an Englishman bound for New York. They talked for a few minutes and both fell into bed.

Wally woke early. He was excited even though he was disappointed with his accommodations. He washed his face in the communal head and again made his way to the deck. The ship had not yet left the dock, but there was a flurry of activity on the dock surrounding the ship. The gangways had been removed and the mooring lines were being cast off. A tug was lined up with the front of the ship and was blowing out black smoke. Wally could feel the ship start to move. He was on his way.

Wally was nervous. The feeling of uneasiness was a rather strange phenomenon for him after all his adventures and close calls, but this was once again a trip into an unknown. At least this time no one would be shooting at him. His stomach was queasy, but he wasn't sick. Some of the other passengers were not so lucky. The ship constantly rolled.

He knew no one in this new country, but he hadn't known anyone at Auschwitz or Stalingrad. He hadn't known anyone in France or on the boat ride over the English Channel. He hadn't known a soul in Scotland, or the first day in the coal mines. He knew no one in Oxford when he went there to paint. He thought of all this and calmed himself. At least Mrs. Bobetska would like the china tea service once he got to Chicago. Would she become a friend?

Wally watched the coast line of England slip behind the ship. The tug was long gone now, and the ship was under its own power. Breakfast was being served in the mess hall. Wally sat at a table with others, but the other passengers seemed to know those close to them and kept their conversations to themselves.

Wally again strolled the decks looking for the Zalas family. He was told on the train that they were in Second Class. Wally was able to find their deck. He stretched out in one of the many lounge chairs and watched as more and more passengers came on deck to watch the departure of their ocean liner.

Before long there was no land in sight. The next piece of real estate would be New York. Wally had heard about the ill-fated ship, *Titanic.* The last piece of land its passengers had seen was a prominent arm of southern Ireland called the Old Head. Wally had no idea what the name of the last piece of land he saw might be named. He just prayed this huge ship would let him see land on the other side of the Atlantic.

The first two days passed with little change in Wally's activities. He was a bit bored. Not a great reader, Wally watched people mingle, but still he did not see the Zalas family. As he sat on the Second Class deck, he saw a young boy, no more than seven, climb onto the railing in front of him and get close to the top. As the child tottered, Wally rushed to the boy and grabbed him, bringing him back down to the deck. One lurch of the ship and the boy would have been gone.

"Oh, my God. Thank you so much," came a woman's voice behind him. As he turned, a middle-aged woman grabbed the boy and began to scold him. The boy was sent to a chair far from the railing and the woman then turned to Wally.

"Thank you, again. We could have lost him. I am Mrs. Pregnitz and that naughty young boy is Peter," the woman said.

"I am Wally Pieszka. Are you going to New York?"

"Well, yes and no. We are landing there but will take a train to Chicago and then make our way to Michigan to a city called Holland," Mrs. Pregnitz replied. A conversation ensued. Wally was ready to talk to someone and the misbehaving boy had become the catalyst.

Soon, Mrs. Pregnitz's husband, Karl, joined the conversation. The family had come from Poland. After the war they had moved to England where their son was born. They, like Wally, had decided to immigrate to America, the land so many people dreamed of as a place to escape war and poverty.

Later that day, Wally met the Zalases on the deck. The three of them talked most of the day. When dinner came, Wally joined them in the mess for the Second Class serving. No one asked him his class of ticket. The staff just assumed that since he was on the Second Class deck, that was his class as well as his companions.

The conversation lasted into the night. Only after that meal did Wally confess that he had traded a Second Class ticket for Tourist in order to get to Chicago sooner. They laughed and spoke of how easily Wally had fit in the other class.

Wally confessed as well about his sleeping quarters in the dormitory. "Get your belongings when you can and put them in our cabin. We have a sitting room with a couch. There is no need to make this journey in a dormitory. Come sleep on our couch," said the gracious Mrs. Zalas.

Since his large suitcases were in storage, Wally carefully made the move with a small suitcase out of the Tourist area and into the sitting room of the Zalas cabin. Life was looking up. He had new friends, old friends and a decent place to sleep and bathe.

Both families stayed in touch with Wally for the next 55 years. He later attended the wedding of that naughty Pregnitz boy, and went to a going-away party for the parents when, after retirement, they chose to move to Belgium in 1992. Both families would visit Chicago for special occasions.

The ten days slipped by quickly. They were to see one bit of land before New York. There was a short stopover at Halifax, Nova Scotia, for an afternoon.

Early on the morning of the tenth day, the skyline of New York appeared on the horizon. As the city came closer, Wally could see landmarks such the Statue of Liberty and the Empire State Building in the distance. Unable to know one tall building from another, Wally was told about each by more seasoned travelers.

After entering the docking area with the assistance of another tug, the *Italia* slid into its berth. Lines were attached and several gangways reached up to the ship. No one left the ship as customs men came aboard and sat at tables near the gangways.

Wally waited his turn, now back in Tourist Class. Each person presented papers which were studied by the man at their gangway. He spent a few moments on each passenger, then stamped several pieces of paper and bid the person a welcome to America. Two photographers standing nearby took pictures of the procedure. Wally looked on with curiosity. He had been across many borders, but never like this. The rest had been in uniform with military papers or as a deserter of the German Army. This was so formal and so proper.

Wally's turn came. He could understand the man's questions but

140

found his accent quite peculiar. Wally had all the right papers, his new British passport and his entry visa. The man looked up to compare his photo on the passport with Wally. Satisfied, he stamped two different pieces of paper and handed them to Wally along with his passport and visa.

Wally walked down the gangplank to America. He felt a rush of excitement. How long ago he had left his real home in Poland and how many different places he had been since then. Secretly he hoped that someday he might be able to at least visit his home country, see his parents and walk the countryside that had been his pleasure before the Germans came.

He found his two suitcases on the dock and inquired where he was to go next. There were several people directing the new arrivals, whether it was to New York or to trains for other parts of this giant country.

Wally spotted the Pregnitz family as they were heading for a bus that would take them to a train station. Wally had read that most immigrants came to a place called Ellis Island, literally an island in the middle of a harbor, but one of the men explained that Ellis Island had been closed a couple of years before. Wally was not to see the Statue of Liberty up close or the Hudson River.

The bus ride was quick ride to a huge place called Grand Central Station. Wally and the Pregnitz family stayed together and soon were directed to a track where they found a waiting train. The railroad car read that it was the New York Central and a sign stated that it was going to Chicago. Wally got a ticket for the train when he bought his ticket for the ship. It was merely for a seat and no overnight accommodations.

Wally and the Pregnitz family entered one of the train cars and chose seats across the aisle from each other. A conductor informed them that an evening meal would be served after departure and that they could eat between 5 and 7:30 p.m.

Once again, Wally settled back into his seat and contemplated what would come next. He would be in Chicago tomorrow morning.

CHAPTER 28

FINDING A JOB

It was early Saturday morning as the train passed through northern Indiana. Wally had no idea that there were so many states between New York and Chicago. As the train passed each state border, the conductor let the passengers know which state was being left behind and which state was being entered. There were several stops in each state. Wally had not heard of many of them.

As the morning sun rose, it shone into the windows. Wally was sitting on the right side and after a while in Indiana, he noticed a large body of water. One of the passengers mentioned that it was Lake Michigan. Wally thought it strange that a lake near Indiana and soon Illinois would be called Michigan. He knew that the Pregnitz family was headed for Michigan, but he didn't know if it was to be near this giant lake or not. The city was called Holland. Again, a strange name for a town so far away from a country of the same name.

In a conversation with the Pregnitz family on the ship, he heard of Holland, Michigan, but that was about it. He got an address and tucked it away in his suitcase. American geography was not yet a strong subject for Wally. He knew that his arrival time was around 10 a.m. and he adjusted his wristwatch to central time. Chicago was fast approaching.

Soon, the train was pulling out of Gary, Indiana, and was weaving past houses and buildings. At almost exactly 10 a.m. the train slowed to a crawl and then entered a darkened area. Wally relaxed, as it was a train station and he could read the name Chicago on a sign.

Wally gathered his two suitcases, one with clothes and one with the tea service for Mrs. Bobetska. He left the train and said goodbye to the Pregnitz family. They were looking for a different train that would take them on to Holland, while Wally was trying to figure out how to find his sponsor. As he walked toward the large entry doors, he saw that it was called Union Station. At least he was in the right place.

As he entered the station, there was a middle-aged lady in a light coat with a sign in her hands that read "Wally Pieszka." She had to be Mrs. Bobetska. As he approached, she could tell that he was her newest charge. She greeted him rather formally and extended her hand.

Wally shook hands and introduced himself. Mrs. Bobetska found a cab and the two entered. "You will have to pay for this ride. It is not included in your tickets, nor is it my job to pay for this trip." She stated this quite flatly, lest there be no mistake.

The ride took about 20 minutes and the fare was $3. Wally had exchanged a few pounds for dollars in New York and was able to pay the cabbie. They were in front of a rather large house with steps leading up to the front door. There seemed to be a few people around, as he heard voices, but no one was on the porch.

Wally and Mrs. Bobetska entered the house, and following her lead, he went down a set of stairs into the basement. Here, Wally saw at least 20 beds in two rows. It was a dormitory!

"The one here on the left is not occupied. There is a foot locker under the bed for your personal items. There is a shower at the end of the room. You will be sharing with 18 men right now. Dinner is at 5. I will leave you to your unpacking," stated Mrs. Bobetska. With that, she left and went up the stairs.

Wally didn't have much to unpack, so he followed behind her. Again he could hear voices of men, and this time he followed the noise to the backyard. There he met several of the other tenants -- a few Poles, a Ukrainian and a couple of Austrians.

It seemed that Mrs. Bobetska had a very profitable business going, and not just for Polish immigrants. On the way to the residence, she explained the procedures of the boarding house and the prices. For $20 a week, he had a place to stay and two meals a day, except Sunday.

Later, dinner was served and most of the men sat at two tables. The food was good, although the food on the boat had been really good. While he didn't miss the boat, he did miss the Pregnitz family. He missed the comraderie of the fellow travelers. Again, Wally was totally alone.

Wally turned in early that night. He was not yet adjusted to the time zone of Chicago. He had plans to visit the city in the morning. He needed a job.

After breakfast, he began to explore his new home on foot. He saw the "Loop" for the first time and noticed a very tall building he later learned was called The Prudential Building. It seemed taller than the others. He walked down Michigan Avenue and State Street, looking in store windows. He was especially impressed with one called Marshall Field's. There were so many huge stores. All were closed for Sunday. This city was like London, but not so old. It was a huge change from Scotland and Oxford. He returned in time for dinner.

Wally awoke early Monday morning and had breakfast in the kitchen. He was told that he needed to register with the Social Security office before he could be properly employed. The nearest office was downtown. Mrs. Bobetska told him in Polish where to catch a bus and what number it would have on its front. The weather was warm, so he needed no coat, and he walked to the nearest bus stop. He was told to have change for the fare and he handed it to the driver. Wally found a seat next to a woman in a very nice suit. She looked quite professional to him, but they did not speak to each other.

After half an hour, Wally could tell that his stop was near. He watched the numbers on the buildings decrease. At number 205, Wally exited the bus and was able to find the right office within a few minutes. The numbering system was far superior to that of London or Kidlington.

He went inside and asked for directions. Once his situation was explained, he was shown to another set of offices and asked to be seated.

After a few moments, Wally was invited into one of the offices. The man there explained the Social Security system and told him he needed to fill out certain papers. He was told that paychecks would have a deduction for this fund and that when he retired, he would receive a monthly benefit.

Wally was asked for his passport, which was now British but with Polish contents. It had been issued after the war to all the Polish soldiers who remained in Scotland or England. He was never sure if his passport was Polish or British, but it seemed to satisfy everyone who saw it, and that document seemed to present no issue with Social Security. Wally received a Social Security number that very morning.

As Wally spoke with the man, he was asked about his skills. It seemed that the man was familiar with a factory that produced certain machines out of metal and that the company was looking for workmen. The man thought there were openings for pipefitters. Wally knew nothing about this occupation but felt he could learn. The company was located on Cicero Avenue, in the village of Cicero. Wally was given the address.

Wally spent some time talking with a woman out front and was able to determine how to get to Cicero where the factory was located. It was called the Donley Machine Company. With that accomplished, he found the bus stop and waited for the right bus to take him to Cicero.

Wally found the factory after asking a few more questions of people on the street and walked in the front door. He was directed to a small employment office where he met the foreman of the factory. He explained to Wally what products they made and how they made them. It seemed that this company made giant presses for the automobile industry. The machines pressed out various automobile parts like fenders, doors and panels. He was told that Donley did not just work for one automaker, but many.

When asked what experience he had, Wally mentioned the coal mine and the various jobs he had there. He indicated that he had worked with pipes and pressure hoses as well as painting. This seemed to interest the foreman, even though he had not yet mentioned work as a pipefitter.

Prior knowledge had helped Wally lead with the right highlight in his oral resume.

The foreman mentioned that the day shift was from 8 to 4. This pleased Wally, as he had always preferred working in the daylight.

There was a cafeteria in the plant and it was a non-union shop. There were no fringe benefits mentioned, but that did not mean much to Wally. He hadn't any such benefits since leaving the military. Wally was told his pay would be $1.85 an hour for a start. This seemed fair for a 40-hour week. Wally indicated his satisfaction with such a rate of pay.

"Mr. Pieszka, can you start tomorrow? We are in real need of some help," asked the foreman.

Wally quickly responded that he would be there. He realized that Mrs. Bobetska' s residence was on Coleman Avenue, north of the Chicago Loop, and this new job was well west of the downtown area. He had to work on the easiest way to get to his new job, but he had a job. Wally again studied the bus schedule and was able to return to the Bobetska home by bus within a little over an hour. He would have to get up early to be prompt.

That evening, Wally sat with Mrs. Bobetska and gave her the china tea settings. She nodded her head but never gave him any thanks. She turned and put the china in her cabinet. Wally was disappointed, after all the work and money he had spent to bring her this gift. Mrs. Bobetska's husband entered the room and saw the china being put away. He looked at the service for a moment, turned and nodded an approval with a smile.

Wally learned the couple had no children. Mr. Bobetska worked at a job outside the house, and Mrs. Bobetska ran the sponsor/boarding house business. She and her husband were both Polish. They had been in America for more than twelve years. They were obviously well known to the British agencies that dealt with immigration.

Several of the men boarding with her came to America after their names were given to Mrs. Bobetska. Whether there was a financial connection was never discovered by Wally. He did learn that all the men brought various gifts to her and were told exactly what to bring.

The evening dinner was served at 6. The men ate together and then either went to the dormitory in the basement or sat in a rather small living room and chatted. Wally decided that he needed companionship and went to the living room. The four or five men there were all Polish, but they all spoke fairly decent English.

Wally was asked a bit of his history. He revealed only that after the war he lived in Scotland and England for almost a dozen years. None of the men had been in the service of any country and seemed to want to know more about Wally's experience, but tonight was not the time.

After a couple of hours, Wally turned in. The lack of privacy reminded him of the first couple of nights on the *Italia*. Tomorrow was an important day, and he went to sleep quickly.

Tuesday morning came with bright sunlight coming in the window. Sunrise was quite similar to Poland, he thought. It woke him before 6 that early July day, and he quickly shaved and washed up. He had some work clothing from his painting days and wore that. There was a quick breakfast, but he had plenty of food since he was one of the first ones up.

Wally mastered the two buses and was at the factory well before 8 a.m. On walking in, he was greeted by a large man with a friendly smile. "My name is Bob. I will be your boss. Come with me and I will show you what you will be doing."

Wally was taken past several large machines to one that was sitting idle. His job would be assembling machines. The work included fabricating parts to fit on or in the machine, then painting and installing them properly. After a few demonstrations, Wally was told to try. It wasn't all that difficult. The foreman watched for several minutes, nodded his head and left Wally at his work. He was back to painting. Soon he was measuring and bending tubing for the oil that flowed through these machines.

Three weeks into his new job, Wally got up for breakfast at his usual time. Normally, he would not read newspapers, even though the *Chicago Tribune* was generally delivered to Mrs. Bobetska's house by 6 a.m. July 27, 1956 was no different.

As Wally was eating breakfast, Mrs. Bobetska slid a newspaper across the table. "Wally, you are one lucky man! Look at the headlines."

There were the headlines in bold, black print. "*Andrea Doria* sinks." The lower, smaller headline read, "40 lost in ocean collision."

Wally sat stunned. That would have been his ship had he gone later from Gibraltar!

Wally read the story as quickly as he could, not wanting to be late for work, but he was intrigued. The newspaper story gave full details.

It seems the *Andria Doria* was sailing to New York City, its destination port, when it collided with the Swedish passenger ship, the *Stockholm*. The *Andrea Doria* sank within minutes of the collision, while the *Stockholm* stayed afloat for several hours.

The collision was close to land, as the two ships were less than 15 miles from New York. Rescue was underway quickly, but since the *Andrea Doria* was listing so badly, half of its life boats could not be lowered. Forty-six people in total were killed in that disaster.

Wally once again thought of his incredible past and his survivals. He had lived through many catastrophes before, and he felt that he would have survived this disaster as well, but everything he owned would have been with him on that ship, including the tea service for Mrs. Bobetska.

At work that day, Wally stayed to himself. He just didn't want to talk. He thought of the travel agent in London wanting to book him on the *Andrea Doria* and how he would have had to go to the continent to catch her. The luxury of that ship was to have been worth it.

Had Mrs. Bobetska not have come through so quickly, he should have been on that tragic sailing.

Wally thought of the disappointment he felt when the *Italia* turned out to be so inferior to what he had been promised if he took the *Andrea Doria*. Then again, he would not have met the Pregnitz family and would not have seen Stefan and Anna Zalas.

When he came home that evening, the entire group was aware of the sinking and Wally's connection with the ship. This time he chose to talk.

He told the story of his choice of ships and why. Later, he spoke of his experiences leading up to England. The group now included Mr. and Mrs. Bobetska and several of the borders.

None of these people had been in the war and no one else had military experience. They pumped Wally for story after story. The group talked almost to midnight. This was not to be a one-time event. Wally became the discussion almost every night.

The job went well, but the commute was a bit long and the Bobetska dormitory was wearing on Wally. There was no privacy, and if Wally arrived late for dinner, there often was nothing left but broth.

Wally decided to find a place of his own. Using the *Chicago Tribune*, he found lists of rentals and finally decided on a basement apartment at 4500 S. Coleman Avenue.

The landlady was Ukrainian and seemed quite happy to have a Pole for a tenant. It wasn't a great apartment, but it was only $40 a month. The landlady lived on the first floor and another tenant had a top attic room.

The location was closer to work, but he noticed that the street in front of the house was quite busy.

As he left the home of Mrs. Bobetska, he was shocked at her attitude. How dare that he leave in just over four weeks? She had assumed that he could not speak English right away and would be forced to stay in the basement for months.

She had used one of her allotted sponsorships on him, and he was cheating her. Wally had no idea that this was a money-making scheme for her, bringing immigrants to Chicago and keeping them for substantial periods of time with high rents for poor accommodations.

Within a week, Wally purchased his first car in America, a used 1956 Plymouth, and he could drive to work. His job with Donley Machine Company lasted almost a year, but after two months of day shifts, Wally was informed that he was being moved to the midnight shift of midnight to 8 a.m. He was assured that it was only temporary.

Wally hated the change. He could not sleep during the day at the

Coleman residence. The traffic was noisy and the other occupants were often moving around when they were not at work. But for now, Donley was a job with decent pay.

As the months went by, Wally's dissatisfaction with the job and especially the midnight shift that wasn't changing led him to look for new employment.

Around the first week of April, 1957, Wally began socializing a bit at local taverns and dances. There he heard a man mention that there were openings at a place called Wrigley. He was not a gum chewer and knew nothing of this name. The job was as a handyman/janitor at the Wrigley building just north of the Chicago River. The hiring was done through an employment office in the Loop. He found the address and made his way to this office.

At the office, Wally was told the pay was $1.85 an hour, and there were benefits from the company including some health coverage and a pension. The work was only day shift. That was a big plus as well. He completed an application form and within a week was hired.

He gave Donley a two-week notice the following day. The boss tried to keep him on board by saying that the midnight shift assignment could be changed, but Wally had heard that tune before. At the end of the two weeks, he departed for work just north of the river.

The work was quite bearable, as he was assigned certain hallways high in the south tower of the Wrigley complex.

He swept and mopped floors, vacuumed offices on that floor, scrubbed down the marble walls and emptied trash.

The hours were good, from 8 a.m. to 4 p.m., six days a week. Wally liked the extra day and was paid overtime for Saturday, a new concept to this Polish man. There were employee meetings once a month, but Wally attended very few.

That spring, his basement apartment flooded from heavy rains. He wondered if it was time to move again. He learned that his old friend, George Kavanagh, from the Kidlington days, followed his lead of emigrating and was now headed for Chicago.

The two had traded letters over the last year. Wally helped find George a sponsor in Chicago, not Mrs. Bobetska, for sure.

George arrived a few months later and made contact with him. They started to spend Saturday nights and Sundays together. George found a job and was living with the family who sponsored him.

The job also was with Wrigley, but was extremely dangerous. The work had George hanging out of windows to make repairs, on top of the building fixing air conditioners, climbing in elevator shafts and entering ventilation ducts. Wally wanted no part of George's job.

There was now serious talk of moving into a new place together.

Later that spring, George and Wally rented a flat in the Bridgeport area. It was on the first floor and was much more spacious. They each had a bedroom, shared a bath and had a kitchen and living room sufficient to meet their needs.

CHAPTER 29

MEETING MARY

Now that he was working in the Wrigley building, his working life became quite regular. He was always on the day shift and had Saturday nights and Sundays off. There was extra money, even though he was still sending some back to Poland and his parents.

Wally and George began to go out socially. There were many dances in the Chicago area. Given the war, most of the men at these dances were younger than the limited number of men who had fought and survived. Wally and George were in the minority as single men in their age group. Most of the eligible women also were much younger.

Wally had been taught to dance by his aunt who had him selling perfume so many years ago. His charm with women from those days was revived. He wanted to meet someone.

George suggested they go to a dance in late May. At first, Wally was hesitant, but he consented. This was to be another life-changing decision.

At the dance, at 63rd and Halsted, there was a woman who seemed a bit older than the other unattached women, and rather shy. Wally approached her and asked her to dance.

"I came with four friends and they are ready to leave," she answered.

Wally persisted. "Oh, I have a car and could give you a lift home later," he responded.

With that, one of the girlfriends said that they could wait a bit longer, and Wally got his dance.

They traded names. "I am Mary Abbeduto." She then awkwardly told him approximately where she lived. They danced several dances, then it was time for her to go.

Wally stalled. "Wait! Can I see you here next Saturday?" he inquired.

"No, I am going on vacation and will be gone for a week," she replied flatly.

Then she quickly explained that she was going to Colorado on a church trip. She was a member of the Catholic church. This news pleased Wally. Cavalierly, Wally asked her to send him a postcard, but she stammered as she turned to go that she didn't know his address. Wally had a pen and paper and quickly gave her his address, removing her excuse and hoping she would comply.

Wally went to work Monday with a new sense of curiosity. He liked this woman. She seemed bright and kind. She was a Catholic and about his age. In his memory, the light bounced off her dark hair. She was very pretty. Would she write to him?

Each evening he checked his mailbox. Nothing. The week dragged on, but he couldn't stop thinking about her. Then on Friday, there it was. A postcard from Colorado. It politely said that the weather was beautiful, and it included her address and phone number. He could not wait to call her Sunday night.

They started seeing each other immediately. His charm was in full swing. Conversations became less awkward as Mary warmed up to him. Their time together included dances, walks along the lake and movies. They rarely ate dinner out, as money was an issue for both. Once a month, he treated her to a restaurant.

They spoke of their respective churches. He learned that she attended the Catholic church regularly, but a different one from Wally. His was on the west side and she lived in Roseland, more south of the city.

Mary had just turned 36, and Wally was 34. To be unwed at the age of 36 was a bit unusual, but the war years had changed American life as it had European life. There were fewer men.

Once again, Wally was the lucky one. There was also an intriguing assortment of ethnic differences, since her parents were of a strong Italian heritage.

After only a few weeks, Mary suggested that he meet her family. Her mother was born in the United States and her father came to America at the age of four months from Italy. His family chose Chicago, as had so many immigrants after the various wars in Europe. Chicago was the ultimate melting pot.

When Wally met the Abbeduto family, he was welcomed with open arms. Acceptance was a far cry from the rejection Wally dealt with back in Poland due to the religious preferences of Regina's mother and the desires of Nancy's father back in Scotland.

Mary had three brothers, Jim, Pat and Louie. The family seemed to really like Wally and included him in all the family events. Wally started to attend church with her. Mrs. Abbeduto treated him like another of her sons. Mr. Abbeduto would probably have preferred an Italian suitor for his only daughter, but was pleased that she had found a decent Catholic man.

They dated regularly and neither saw anyone else. Less than a year later, Wally surprised Mary with a request to walk to the park. There he opened a small box he had in his pocket. He solemnly told Mary how much he loved her, and he asked her to be his wife.

Tears trickled down her cheek, and she was able to nod and quietly say yes. They hugged and left for the Abbeduto home. Wally needed Mr. Abbeduto's permission to marry his daughter.

When Wally asked for her hand in marriage, a fear of any hesitation by the father was quickly dispelled.

"I would consider it an honor, Wally. You are and will be family. But you must make sure that all is in order with our priest."

Shortly after, there was a meeting with Mary's priest. It did not go well.

"I must have proof that you are Catholic," the priest insisted.

Wally assured him that he was, but all of his proof and papers were back in Poland. He even raised the point that had he not been a Catholic, he would have ended up dead or in Auschwitz or some similar place. The priest would not back down.

In frustration, Wally wrote his old priest in Ilownica, Father Niemuk. Wally hoped that the man was still alive and able to help him. He was not disappointed, as his old mentor came through immediately.

Within two weeks, the papers arrived, but in Polish. Whether the Italian priest had them translated, or because he knew some Polish, was never revealed, but the priest consented to marry Wally and Mary.

The date of May 31, 1958, was chosen.

Meanwhile, Wally was still at his janitorial job. His pay remained $1.85 an hour, but overtime was common.

The problem was that the union dues subtracted from his check each week aggravated Wally. He felt neither a need nor affection for this union. The Wrigley Company was already treating them well, with many benefits. Wally stuck it out, as it was steady work in a decent environment and his wedding was coming.

Mary had been working for a men's clothier, Joseph Levin, on South Wentworth in the city. She was a bookkeeper for Mr. Levin and would work there more than 33 years. Wally would eventually get his ties, shirts, and on occasion, a suit from Mary's employer. Mr. Levin, a Russian Jew who had come to the United States before the war, specialized in high-end men's fashion. Not quite the style of clothing Wally wore, but on occasion Wally enjoyed wearing the clothing from Levin's.

Wally and Mary were to be married at St. Anthony's Catholic Church. George Kavanagh agreed to be his best man, and all three of Mary's brothers were groomsmen. The bridesmaids were Mary's friends from the dance where they met.

The Zalas family came, as did the Pregnitz family from Michigan.

Wally asked the Zalases to act as his parents, as none of his family would be permitted to leave Poland to attend the ceremony. George

152

took over as the best man should, but Wally worried about George. His drinking was becoming much heavier. While his war experiences were nothing compared to Wally's, he had bouts of depression and often drank heavily during these times. He had been Wally's best friend since working together in Oxford. He was glad that George decided to come to Chicago, but he was still concerned about George.

The wedding day came on May 31, 1958. The couple had known each other for just eight months, but both of them were older and felt their decision to wed was based on love.

Time was most important if they were to have a family. Both knew this decision was right. Their love for each other was apparent to both friends and families. The short period of time was never an issue.

The wedding was huge, with 200 for a breakfast and 300 attending the wedding. Even Mr. Levin and his wife attended. The church was packed for the ceremony and a full Mass at 11:00 that morning.

The temperature soared to 90 degrees, but the inside of the old church stayed cool for the ceremony. The men, waiting in the wings, however, began to sweat and couldn't wait for the proceedings to begin. The priest who had put Wally though rigorous questioning and demand for papers, performed the ceremony.

After the ceremony and reception, the couple slipped away. It was their first private night completely alone together. Their courting had been quite pure to date. The honeymoon was not that far away, and they spent the week at a place called the Wagon Wheel, a few miles southwest of Chicago.

Upon his marriage, Wally left the Bridgeport apartment and George. George decided to go back to his sponsor's apartment while Wally and Mary found an apartment to rent on 115th Street in Roseland, another small community in south Chicago. It was above a furniture store and needed a lot of work. Over the next few months, Wally painted the entire apartment, repaired molding, and fixed a few plumbing problems. Their first nest was now comfortable and cozy.

Within a few months of their marriage, George announced his own engagement to Nuala Gorski. Wally returned the favor and acted as best man for George. George and Nuala soon returned to Ireland for several years before coming back to the United States. They later decided to go to California, and the friendship was continued only by the occasional letter.

After only a few months, the new couple's landlady visited the Pieszka's newly decorated flat. She marveled at the job Wally and Mary had done and within a month raised the rent! Wally was furious.

The search was on, and within a month the couple decided to buy a small house in the Wentworth area. It was newly built and had had no occupants yet.

It was like they had built their own home. Their new address was 10507 103rd Street.

The First National Bank looked with favor on the couple and their employment. A loan was secured for $19,000 and the house was bought.

Wally often wondered whether they would have had a different history of housing had that former landlady not raised the rent.

They lost some money on the repairs and improvements for the rented flat, but Wally and Mary now owned a house of their own.

CHAPTER 30

THE WRIGLEY JOB

As a janitor, Wally received notices of all monthly union meetings. In the first few months he felt no compunction to attend, but later in the fall of 1958, he heard of the agenda for the coming meeting. It concerned an effort to force the Wrigley Company to accept a new contract. Wally decided to attend.

That Sunday night, there were nearly a hundred men in attendance at the union hall. The speakers complained that Wrigley was not being fair to them and there might be a need to strike, as the two sides were far apart on the signing of a union contract.

The second speaker, a high union official, explained the two positions. Wally was astounded at what the union was demanding. Wrigley was already giving many benefits and, in Wally's opinion, all the union would do was charge him dues.

There came a time when the floor was opened for comment. Much to his own surprise, Wally went to the microphone.

"I think you are wrong with your demands. What Wrigley pays us now is more than fair. I have worked in factories, coal mines and on the farm. This is by far the best job I have ever had. We even get our birthday off with pay. We should all be thankful for the Wrigley Company and what they have offered us. We should not strike."

He sat down. There were a few boos. Wally walked to the back of the hall. There a woman approached him and said that it might be best if he left as soon as he could.

There were several union members unhappy with what he had said, and he heard talk of them beating him up. Wally left immediately without any confrontation.

The next day he reported as usual for work. Later in the day, the foreman approached him. "You are to go up to the 16th floor and report to Mr. Butler."

Wally was nervous. The 16th floor was for top executives. Was he in trouble for his comments the night before?

Wally arrived at the 16th floor and asked for Mr. Butler. He was told to take a seat. The wait was about ten minutes or so when a well-dressed man approached him and asked if he was Mr. Pieszka. He replied that he was and was asked to follow him.

They walked into another office with another man sitting at a large desk.

"I am Mr. Butler. I work directly for Mr. P.K. Wrigley. Mr. Pieszka, it has come to our attention that you spoke up at the union meeting last night." Wally swallowed hard and nodded that he had and was about to apologize, when Mr. Butler said, "We are offering you a job directly with the company."

"You have been selected to work here inside the building. You have demonstrated a satisfaction with Wrigley that most of those other workers don't hold. It was noticed and brought to our attention. Would you like to work here?"

Wally always hoped for a more important job than a laborer. He spent years in the coal mines before he found a niche in painting. He had enjoyed being self-employed, but the management aspects were not that easy for him. His work in the metal industry and as a janitor had made him a wage, but there hadn't been much satisfaction in those jobs either.

As he sat there, he wasn't actually clear on what he would be doing, but those around the 16th floor were wearing ties and jackets. That alone made an impression about the working area he was being asked to join.

Wally said he would like such a job before he even learned the particulars or the wages.

"You will be working in a small department that supplies all the paper products to the top floors. You will also have various other duties. Mr. P.K. Wrigley's office is nearby, and his needs must be met if anything arises. He is the main man here. There is a room on 17 that will be your assigned area. You will work with another Pole. His name is Kolodziejski. There are five other people in the department. "

When his wages were explained, he realized that this was an improvement over his janitorial job. Better dress, better people, better money and good benefits. Wally responded that he would have to talk to his wife.

That night he shared the news with Mary. He explained that he would be working directly for the company, whether a strike occurred or not. The wages were to be as good, and there would be steady raises. He shared with her that he liked the idea of dressing up each day, but that he would need more jackets, even though ties were not a problem. She was excited with the offer and they agreed he would accept the job the next day.

The following day, Wally reported to the same receptionist. He was expecting to see Mr. Butler. The receptionist directed him to the supply room as though everyone knew he was taking the job. There he met his boss, Ted Kolodziejski. There were five other people working in the supply room, three Poles and two blacks.

The job was a bit routine each day. Wally handed out supplies, ran errands, and made sure he followed his boss's orders. The pay was as good as being a janitor, but with fewer deductions.

He needed to dress differently. He now wore a tie every day, which came from Mr. Levin at a very reasonable price. Often, his fellow workers would ask how he could afford such nice ties. Eventually, he let on that his prices were quite reasonable under the circumstances. Not only were his co-workers jealous, they wanted to know if he could help them out. He politely declined. There was no way he would threaten the relationship he and his wife had with Mr. Levin.

Wally watched with a bit of awe as Ted, his boss, often talked with Mr. P.K. Wrigley. Both seemed at ease, as though neither was a boss.

Phillip Knight, or P.K. Wrigley as he was known, was the son of William Wrigley, the founder of the chewing gum empire. In 1932, William died, leaving his son the chewing gum business, various real estate properties, a piece of Santa Catalina Island and the newly purchased Chicago Cubs.

P.K. took the responsibility of owning the Cubs quite seriously, and he felt that this ownership had special sentimental value as well as financial importance. P.K. was quoted as saying, "I will never dispose of my holdings in the club as long as the chewing gum business remains profitable enough to retain it."

One day, Wally received an unusual request. Could he go to the president's office, Mr. P.K. Wrigley? Wally was apprehensive, but quickly went down the hall to the private office of this well-known Chicago business magnate.

"What is your name again?" Mr. Wrigley asked. Wally told him and pronounced it twice.

"Well, I have been looking for someone to help me straighten my office. I am considering slowing down a bit and letting my son, Bill, take over." Now Wally had officially met "the man."

Wally was to learn over time and through many conversations quite a lot about his boss. While P.K. ran the business side of his holdings quite profitably, owning the Chicago Cubs was different. The baseball side confused him. P.K. once said, "Baseball is too much of a sport to be a business, and too much of a business to be a sport."

Over the years, reaping profits and minimizing expenses seemed to rule his priorities. The team often suffered with bad trades and holdout players. The major leagues finally integrated in 1947. The Cubs signed their first black players in1953, when Gene Baker and Ernie Banks joined the club.

Wrigley seldom had a winning season with his club, but he was attempting to promote the fun of the game over winning. The Cubs lost for years.

Wally began helping Mr. Wrigley straighten out the office and the matters necessary for the changing of the presidency.

As P.K.'s role diminished, he had more free time, and he often invited Wally into his office to merely sit and talk.

Wally, over time, shared some of his World War II stories. He also shared his life in Poland before the war. Mr. Wrigley always seemed fascinated with these stories.

Mr. Wrigley shared stories of his own. He told Wally that his wife, Helen, had been in a coma for many years. He talked about some of his loneliness at home. He also shared many stories of his ownership of the Chicago Cubs and his love of the game.

A very special relationship was developing. It was a bit unusual, a business giant in the twilight of his career sharing somewhat private information with a Polish immigrant-employee.

CHAPTER 31

LOSING A DAUGHTER

Life for the newlyweds continued at a hectic pace. Wally's job with Mr. Wrigley was working out well, though the hours were long. Mary loved her job with the Levin Company. She was an important cog in their business and felt needed. Then she threw up.

It started in the morning before she arose and lasted almost all day. Her breasts were sore and she lost her appetite. All this meant nothing to Wally. Then she mentioned she was "late." Wally suddenly understood. It was time to find a doctor.

There was a family doctor associated with the Roseland Hospital and his office was close to their home. Mary had no sisters or close friends who could go with her to that first appointment, so the day and time were picked for Wally to attend. It was on a Wednesday evening.

Both sat nervously in the waiting room as they waited their turn. Soon, they were ushered into the doctor's office. Mary explained her symptoms. Dr. Esau smiled and said that there was a test that could confirm a pregnancy, but he was pretty sure that Mary was expecting. He sent her to a room where she could give a urine sample, and they sat a few more minutes in the waiting room before the doctor came out and announced that there was a baby coming.

Both were ecstatic. Mary was not young to be a first-time mother, and Wally wondered what it would like to be a father after all these years. They calculated that the baby would come in late spring or early summer of 1959.

Both went back to work, made the monthly visits to the doctor, and thought about parenthood. Unfortunately, Mary was not comfortable. She knew that there would be discomfort and the morning sickness did subside, but she was just uncomfortable almost all the time. The doctor assured her on the visits that all was fine and she was progressing well.

The fall quickly became a Chicago winter. Both Mary and Wally trudged through heavy snow to work and to the doctor. Spring and a baby were coming.

Around the first of March, Mary was getting fairly large and was still uncomfortable. The doctor continued to believe that all was fine. It was a Saturday, and while Wally generally worked each Saturday, he was home the afternoon of March 4, 1959.

Mary called to Wally. "It's happening, Wally. I think the baby is coming!"

Wally knew the dates they thought the child would come, but this was too early. "Are you sure?" he asked.

"I am sure. Get me to the hospital."

Wally quickly got ready to go and hustled Mary into the family car. The drive to Roseland Community Hospital was short. Wally pulled up to the emergency door dropped her off with the nurses and went to park the car. There were no spaces. He drove away from the hospital doors and finally found a spot to park.

He hurried to the emergency door. As soon as he entered, one of the nurses approached him, "You have a baby girl!"

Wally stood in shock. How could it happen so fast? He heard that labor could take hours and hours. The doctor wasn't even there.

Mary was in a room, but the baby was in a separate place. The nurse then confided to Wally, "She is quite premature and is struggling. You can see her through the glass, but she needs a lot of special care. Dr. Esau is on his way."

Wally peeked at the tiny infant through the glass and then found a seat in the waiting room. In a few moments, Dr. Esau appeared. "Wally, we have some problems. Your daughter is quite premature. Perhaps a month and a half. She only weighs three and half pounds. She is too weak to be with Mary, so we will keep her here in a special care area."

The news seemed to just bounce off Wally's ears. This was not how it was planned. He needed to see Mary. The nurses said she was able to have him visit and they showed him down the hall to her room. Obviously, the doctor had not shared all the grim news.

"Mary, the little girl is struggling. She is so early. Dr. Esau is worried." Mary just stared ahead.

"We have to name her," she murmured more than she spoke. "We will call her Kathleen."

Wally quickly agreed. Mary inquired whether she could see her baby, but Wally informed her that it was impossible for the moment. "We have to have her baptized, at least," Mary insisted.

Wally again agreed and said he would find the parish priest as soon as he could.

Wally stayed a while. He could see that Mary was tired. He quietly slipped out of the room and decided it was time to find the priest. He drove to the church and quickly found Father Slovak.

"Father, I think you need to come to Roseland Hospital. My baby daughter is struggling and we want her baptized just in case something happens." The priest wasted no time.

Wally drove the two of them to the hospital. Surprising to Wally, the nurses permitted Father Slovak to enter the nursery room and actually touch the baby as he performed the rite of baptism.

Wally drove the priest back to the church. Father Slovak tried to offer words of encouragement, but Wally couldn't find any peace. In his heart, he knew things were bad. He had a feeling of doom, much like those days in Stalingrad.

He dropped off the priest and realized he had not shared the news with Mary's family. A quick trip to their house found no one at home, so he returned to the hospital and spent the evening with Mary, often checking with nurses as to Kathleen's condition. Finally, he went home and collapsed into bed.

The next morning, he went to Mass at 7 and then went directly to the hospital. Mary was better but still upset she couldn't see her daughter. By now, Mary's family had received the news of the birth by telephone, and Mary's brother, Jim, came to the hospital to sit with Wally and Mary. Nothing had changed, and again Wally and Jim went home.

Wally called into work and was assured he need not come in. He returned to the hospital and things seemed to have changed. The nurses were less talkative. Mary was more alert, but unsettled, as well.

About 9:30, Jim came in and the three sat in Mary's room. Then Wally was summoned to the nursery. There was Dr. Esau.

"We have decided that we need to transfer your daughter to Michael Reese Hospital. It is better equipped to deal with premature infants. She will go by ambulance."

Wally and Jim watched as the tiny infant was wrapped in blankets and placed in an ambulance. The two of them followed the ambulance in Wally's car. Once there, they were told that the infant was in the critical care portion of the hospital for infants and there really wasn't anything the men could do but wait. They would stay in touch by telephone.

Jim and Wally drove back to the Roseland hospital. Wally went in to see Mary and brought her up to date, and then he went home to sleep.

The next day was no different. He saw Mary and then drove to Michael Reese. The nurses were grim but offered some hope as he spoke to them. They encouraged him to go home. Wally returned to the Roseland hospital and then went home.

The following morning, March 7, the telephone rang. It was early but Wally hadn't slept much anyway. He did not recognize the voice on the phone nor did the woman identify herself. She merely stated that she was from Michael Reese Hospital.

"Mr. Pieszka, I am sorry to inform you that we lost your daughter early this morning. If you need any help with arrangements with funeral personnel, we can provide names of local funeral homes."

With that, the conversation was over, as was the life of his first child.

Mary still had not seen her daughter, and it would remain that way. Wally was told to see a funeral director named Panozzo and was given an address. Upon seeing one of the directors, arrangements were made to pick up the tiny body at the hospital and deliver it to the funeral home.

Mr. Panozzo met with Wally personally. He explained that there needed to be a casket and a cemetery lot. Wally chose the Abbeduto family cemetery and was told that there was a special section for infants. He consented to the arrangements and left to go tell Mary the news.

Mary cried and Wally held her as he explained what had happened and the funeral plans. He assured her that they would try to have another baby; that they would not stay childless.

Wally knew that Mary was anxious about her age and childbearing, but they quietly agreed that they could try again.

The next day, while Mary remained in the hospital, Jim and Wally met with Mr. Panozzo. They drove in Jim's car to the cemetery and met the hearse as instructed. Two of the Panozzo employees carried the small coffin to the grave. It had been dug the evening before, and while very small, it was quite deep.

The casket was lowered into the ground with only the two Panozzo men, plus Wally and Jim. There was no priest.

The burial was over in just a few moments. Jim drove Wally back home and the day was done.

Wally knew that life needed to go on again in spite of the tragedy.

CHAPTER 32

A SON, CITIZENSHIP, AND A RETURN

Wally and Mary went back to work, and within a few weeks regular life resumed. Mr. Wrigley offered baseball tickets to Wally, perhaps trying to cheer him up, but there was no time in his life for sports. Instead Wally went to work on the newly-built house on Wentworth Avenue.

Since there was now a mortgage to pay for the first time, household income didn't go as far, but with both working, bills were paid on time. Somewhere in those hard working times, Wally and Mary had time for romance and even several evenings out or with her family.

In 1960, Mary was again pregnant. This time the pregnancy went well. Mary announced that it was time to go to the hospital. Wally had been home that day, as it was a Sunday. He was painting the garage when Mary announced that her water had broken.

Wally dropped Mary off at the emergency room door and went to park the car at the Roseland hospital. There were no spaces to be found, so he circled the parking lot again and again. Finally, there was a space. He parked and walked quickly to the entrance.

A nurse met him at the door to the emergency room and announced, "Mr. Pieszka, you have a baby boy."

Twice now he hadn't made it from the parking lot to the emergency room before his child was born. This time, however, it was a joyous occasion, as the emergency room doctor announced that the baby boy was healthy and weighed almost eight pounds. What a change from a year and a few months ago.

The child was named Wally after his father, although not the Polish spelling. Within five days, the son and mother were home.

Mary took off a few months from work with the complete blessing of Mr. Levin. When she did return, she went back just part time. She was now a mother with a child. Wally's hours did not change, as he still worked many Saturdays.

To the surprise of Wally, soon after the birth a package for the newborn came from old Scottish friend, Mrs. Torschak. While correspondence had been sparse, Wally stayed in touch with her over the years.

The area of the Wentworth home was not as nice as they had hoped after moving from Roseland. There were more and more people who did not seem to care about their community or themselves. Crime became more common. Someday not all that far away, young Wally would start school. While his parents talked of a Catholic school, tuition meant extra money. After serious discussion, the couple decided that life was going fairly well. They could think more about a move as young Wally grew.

While Mary's family home had been a bit more spacious, this was the largest home Wally had ever lived in. Mary was happy with her son and loved her job with Mr. Levin. Wally's work went well at Wrigley. P.K. Wrigley seemed to be working less and had more time to talk to Wally.

Once again, P.K. gave baseball tickets to him for the special seats the family had as owners of the Chicago Cubs. Wally now chose to accept them, but luck was not so good. On three separate occasions when Wally had the tickets, those Sunday games were rained out.

He had become a British citizen in 1950 having spent five years in Scotland after the war ended. Now that he was married to an American woman and had an American son, perhaps it was time to become an American himself. Clearly there was no thought of returning to England. Poland was also not a possibility under the present regime.

Wally inquired about the procedure in becoming a naturalized citizen of the United States in October of 1961. He had been in the country long enough and was employed. He learned that he would have to make an application and then take a test on American law and its governmental structure. This test was to be followed by an oral interview.

Wally obtained the necessary study material. For several weeks, he read about his new country's history and political structure. He felt ready for the test.

He made the trip to the Federal Building in downtown Chicago in early January, where he sat for the written test. He found the test rather easy and was quickly informed that he had passed. The interview followed a few minutes later. Again he was successful with this part of the procedure and was told that he would be notified of the official proceeding for naturalization by mail.

The letter came within a week and informed him to be back at the Federal Building on February 20. Wally went alone to the event, as Mary stayed with young Wally. His brothers-in-law would have attended, but Wally wanted to do this alone and there was no need for them to take off work.

On February 20, 1962, Wally entered the court room as directed. There was a judge sitting on the bench, but Wally did not learn his name. The judge announced to the 20 or so candidates that there would be an oath given to them. If they had chosen to change any part of their name, they should respond with that new name. Wally decided to change his official first name from Wladyslaw to Walter, and he responded with that new name.

There were quite a few family members of the other applicants in the back of the court room, and they clapped loudly after the judge finished and congratulated them on becoming American citizens.

Wally returned home that day with his signed certificate of naturalization in his new name. The document was signed by Roy H. Johnson, the clerk of the District Court of Illinois.

Within a few weeks, Wally received a personal letter from Edwin Derwinski, the congressman from Wally's district at the Wentworth address, and a fellow Pole.

Apparently, politics did not rest. He was a new voter. Now Wally and his family were Americans, all with the right to vote.

Life seemed always at a hectic pace. Two parents, both with jobs. A son growing by leaps and bounds. But there was one part of Wally's life that seemed to tear at his heart.

With the approach of the year 1963, it had been twenty years since he had seen his parents or brothers Frank and Emil. It had been 18 years since he had seen Andrew.

There had to be a way to get to Poland, even though it continued to be under Communist control. He decided to pursue this yearning. He would need time off from work and some extra money.

Mary stated quite firmly that with young Wally, she could not and did not want to go. She did understand her husband's need to see his parents and brothers, and she encouraged him to look into such a trip.

In early 1963, Wally started to pursue a trip to Poland in earnest. First, he approached P.K. about taking some substantial time off. P.K. agreed to a month and word went down the line that this could occur in the coming summer.

The first step was complete, as he could not afford to lose his job, especially since he would be digging into savings to make such a visit. Mary and he talked for several weeks. He still wanted his wife to go. She had never met any of his family and her family had treated him like a son. He knew his family would treat her similarly.

They had long discussions, but in the end there was no way they could take young Wally, nor could they leave him for a month. He was a baby. After some heart-wrenching talks, it was finally decided that Wally would go alone.

Wally had been exchanging letters with his parents and Emil for years now. If he could get to Warsaw or Krakow, they could find a way to house him and feed him at no cost. Wally needed only the transportation money and costs of visas. He had his American passport since he became a U.S. citizen.

Now the trick was to find a safe but inexpensive way. In search ing the newspapers, Wally found a tour leaving Chicago and arriving in Warsaw with an extended stay and a tour for a full month. He didn't want a tour of his own country, but perhaps they could help with the transportation and regulations visiting a Soviet bloc country.

That Saturday, he went to downtown Chicago and visited the travel agency that had run the ad in the *Chicago Tribune*.

The trip became simple. The agency could help him with the visa for Poland and could provide the air transportation. He didn't have to take the land portion of the tour. He only had to pay the transportation portion. The price was affordable and the departure time fit Wally's plans. He was set.

By the first of May, Wally paid the agency and was directed to the Polish consulate. The paperwork was prepared for him by the agency and a visa was issued for the dates involved. He thought there would be more involved, but the only problem encountered was the time lapse between applying and receiving the visa.

It took almost three weeks to get the document back. By the time he received his paperwork, there were only two weeks before departure.

Letters were again exchanged with his Polish family. The plane was to be met by Emil in Warsaw upon arrival. The entire family would be in Ilownica to greet him. In one of the letters, Wally was told by Emil that to make such a trip by a Polish man trying to visit the United States could take up to six months to arrange and the price was exorbitant. It was good to be an American.

With kisses and hugs, Mary accompanied Wally to the gate at O'Hare airport for his departure. He was nervous. The stories of life behind the "Iron Curtain" were disturbing, but he wanted to see his family.

Jet aircraft for overseas flights was rather new, Pan Am having initiated service to Europe in 1957. Wally was set to fly in his first jet, a Boeing 707, non-stop to Warsaw, Poland.

There was only one class of tickets on this chartered flight. The passengers sat three seats on each side of the aisle. There were more than 100 people on the airplane.

Wally, by chance, got the window seat. It seemed that all the travelers were Polish or had Polish roots. Polish was the language of the day.

The flight seemed to go on forever. The seats were not that comfortable, but the food was excellent. For a long part of the flight, Wally stared out the window in mild amazement. They were flying incredibly high and the ocean seemed to go on forever. The couple beside him spoke Polish and invited him to join in their conversation, but Wally's mind was elsewhere.

As morning broke, Wally saw land. Europe unfolded in front of him. Perhaps it was France. He had made one short trip to France by boat with his friend and former employee, George Kavanaugh, since coming to England in 1943. From the air, there was nothing he could recognize. The airplane droned on.

After several hours of flying over terrain of mountains and plains, rivers and lakes, an announcement came over the loudspeaker from the captain, but not the announcement everyone expected. They had been circling over Poland for thirty minutes, but had not descended.

"This is the Captain. We have been denied permission to land in Warsaw. There are some difficulties with getting permission, and we have been told to turn back and land somewhere else. We cannot land in Poland. We have chosen Copenhagen as our new destination and should be there in less than two hours. You will receive further instruction upon landing."

Wally later learned that some of his family had waited at the Warsaw airport for several hours, but were told nothing and traveled back home by train.

Meanwhile, upon landing in Copenhagen, the passengers were told that prepayment of the landing fee at Warsaw had not been paid and their flight was rejected. Having never flown before on such a trip, Wally did not know what to make of this statement.

The passengers were offered two options. An airplane properly booked and cleared could leave within two hours, but there would be an extra charge. The travel agency was not picking up any part of the charge. Wally felt he could not afford this choice.

The second option was that they could be taken to a train station, and with two changes of trains, the passengers could arrive in Warsaw later the next day. He made the latter choice, while most opted to fly, as the group's travel plans could commence earlier and stay on schedule.

Wally was transported by bus to the train station and was able to book a train within three hours. The trip lasted all night and into the afternoon of the following day. He was given a new ticket for his return flight, but again this was to be from the Copenhagen airport, not Warsaw.

There was no way to communicate these changes in plans to the Pieszka family, and he arrived in Warsaw to find no one there for him. Some things hadn't changed that much, though.

Within an hour, Wally was on a train with one change all the way to Chybie. The scenery was familiar and this time Wally recognized the surrounding landscape as he looked out the window. They went past Krakow and then Bielsko. There, he changed trains and arrived in Chybie a few minutes past 6 p.m.

It was summer and there was plenty of light.

How many times he had walked or ridden his bicycle from this town to his home in Ilownica he could not count. But not this time. Wally hired a taxi to make the drive and was at the house in Ilownica before 8.

As he approached his old home, Wally felt a mix of emotions. Other than photographs, he had never seen this home although it sat on the same location and on the same foundation as the home he had left in 1942. It was beautiful by Polish standards.

His mother had spoken to Wally about ceding any rights he had in this home to his brother, Emil, on the event of his parents passing and Wally not being a Polish resident. His house? He could not return to this Poland. His position and experience at Wrigley would not transfer any skills that could relate to another decent paying occupation, although he thought about it.

Wally hesitated at the door. Should he knock or walk in? He chose not to knock and the door was not locked.

As he entered the hallway and the living room, he saw that the family was still gathered together. There were his parents, and Emil and Sophie and their children, Mary and Janek (who later became John).

The first to rush him was his mother, who cried as she hugged her long-lost son. His father firmly shook his hand in spite of the old railroad injury. This was followed by smiles and shouts of greeting from the rest of the family.

Wally was hungry. His mother quickly prepared a feast from the food that had been saved from the day before. He explained his delay and the trip backward to Copenhagen and assured them that he still had almost a month before his return.

The next day, his personal tour of his old homeland started in earnest. With different members of the family, Wally visited Ilownica, Chybie and his old haunts. His "new" school was still the school. Buildings were similar, but much older. Some were just gone and not rebuilt. There were few cars now. His family still didn't own one. The houses were more modern with more electrical gadgets and lighting.

One special trip was to see his old priest, Father Niemuk. With him they visited the family cemetery and the graves of family and friends.

He and Father Niemuk discussed their talk in 1942 when he was about to be drafted. They recounted the old priest's advice and blessing. The priest seemed pleased that his advice had led to a good life for Wally. In spite of the many challenges and suffering, Wally had endured.

Wally again thanked him for that life-saving advice given some 20 years before. Wally attended several of Father Niemuk's Masses during his stay in the very church in which he had been raised. He marveled that in spite of the strict governmental control of the state and the lives of the Polish people, the services were in Latin.

Within a few days, Wally met his brothers, Frank and Andrew, and their families. Both lived in different villages but not far from Ilownica. While each had a good job, his brothers had not been allowed to excel in their various professions. The governmental regulations kept everything under strict control. Wally thought of his own life, his ability to change jobs, to spend money as he wished and to buy things that were not even offered in Poland. None of his family even had a telephone.

Soon the month passed. There were numerous pleasures and some disappointments. His old savior, Mrs. Kopec, had died and her home had been demolished. The family of his first romantic encounter was gone, as was their home. There was joy and sadness each day. While he knew he had made the right decision to not return so many years ago, his heart still ached for his family and the neighborhood of his youth.

However, it was time to go home to his family and America.

With the entire family at the Chybie railway station waving good-bye, Wally started his trip back to Krakow, Warsaw and eventually Copenhagen. On his arrival at the airport, the airplane for his departure was ready, but the staff informed him that the company was not going to refund any airplane or travel expenses. Wally felt good that he had once again chosen frugally.

Before he departed, his mother once again said, "If something happens to father, there is a problem with the house under the present laws. It will go to the state." He couldn't let this happen to his family. She wanted him to assign his rights to Emil.

Wally thought about all this on his plane trip back to the United States. He knew that the house and land was worth a fair amount of money. But Emil had been the one son of his mother who had stayed with her and her husband since the war. He helped rebuild the home when it burned down in 1945, and started a business in the building next to the house. He was the sole caregiver for their mother and Wally's father. He would sign the papers to give up his ownership in the property.

The airplane ride was similar. He again had a window seat. This time, all the passengers were more talkative. They discussed what they had seen and almost everyone shared the sadness of seeing their old country under the Soviet rule. Poland was once again not Poland. Whether ruled by the Austrians, the Germans, or now the Russians, it was an occupied country. The rules of a foreign power were again imposed on this beleaguered nation of hardworking and proud people.

The fellow visitors commented on the lack of true opportunity for their relatives or friends in Poland. Many had spoken earnestly with the citizenry that they had visited. Freedom of religion was once again under siege. Education was controlled by a foreign government. Affiliation in the Communist Party was essential to strive and even survive. Roads were not improved. Very few citizens had a private car or truck. Housing was rather minimal and most work was done by the owner and family, as there was

169

no money for skilled labor. Private ownership was there, but limited. There were no bank loans or mortgages.

The socialist state was "Big Brother," but this brother was not very generous.

As Wally stepped off the airplane in Chicago, he wanted to kiss the ground of his new nation. There was his wife with his son in her arms, with their car in the parking lot, which would take them to their own personal and exclusive residence.

After the last month, this was paradise. He was home, and any desire to return to live in his country of birth was gone forever. Wally Pieszka was an American.

Shortly after his return to the Wentworth home, paperwork arrived, all in Polish, and Wally could read it. It was a surrender of his rights in the home. The papers had to be in place before his father died. He signed them and with a short note, mailed them to his mother.

CHAPTER 33

THE DEATH OF
HIS PARENTS

The 1963 visit to Poland and his family seemed so long ago. Wally missed certain things about his homeland, but communism and the Soviet state were not among them.

One big change was with the attitude of the people. These hard working rural people were being placed in more commercial industry. No longer was there a need for all the sons to stay on the farm. Jobs were always available because of high turnover, as many were routine and repetitive. Most jobs paid the same anyway. Luxury items were non-existent. Few people had cars.

Wally had just bought his first brand new car, a 1964 Plymouth Valiant, and his old Plymouth was history. He wrote to his family of the purchase but was careful not to elicit envy. When Wally was in Ilownica in 1963, he realized how much he came to depend on a car for daily life.

In the summer of 1968, Wally was at work and was exhausted after his return home. Mary met him at the door with a telegram in her hand. Wally knew it was bad news before he even opened it. It was from his mother. His father had died three days before and the funeral was over by the time Wally was informed of the death.

While it was not unexpected, the fact that a man's father could pass away and his son would not be able to arrange a passage to his funeral stung. The paperwork to go to Poland would have taken weeks; such was the state of the Soviet Bloc and the United States. The Cuban missile crisis was still fresh in the minds of the two countries, where nuclear war had been narrowly averted.

A few weeks later a letter explained more about his father's death and his funeral. The service was conducted by Father Niemuk, and that fact gave Wally some peace. The letter also informed him that Emil now owned the house. The transfer was complete.

His family in Poland seemed as far away as the moon. Letters were exchanged with some regularity, but there was no telephone available with families such as his. In addition, the cost of transportation from one country to the other was almost completely prohibitive for working class people. As much as Wally wanted to see his mother to provide mutual comfort, it just couldn't happen.

Life went on in the community of Wentworth. Wally's friend, George Kavanagh, returned to the United States from Ireland. Wally saw him a few times before George moved to California, but noticed that George was even more obsessed with drinking since his return. In fact, when the two couples were together, both George and his wife would become intoxicated by the end of the evening. While Wally had no problem with a social drink or two, George seemed to need much more than that on a regular basis and the need had become worse.

After George left Chicago for California, the friendship cooled. The Pregnitz family was in the country, but in Michigan. Stephan and Anna Zalas were busy sending money to Poland and wondering if they should return there someday.

Again Wally had his family, Mary's family and work. Friends were limited. Mary was still working part time for Raymond Levin and Wally continued to be one of the best-dressed men at Wrigley.

In late 1969, there was another telegram. This time Emil sent it. Mother had passed away earlier that week. Letters followed as before, but once again politics and money kept families from joining together in these times of grief.

Wally vowed another trip back home to Ilownica before his brothers all died. His family was steadily shrinking.

But even in America, life was complicated. There was a son to raise and direct on the positive path. Thoughts of college someday for young Wally replaced thoughts of another trip to Poland.

Wally was now parentless, something that usually happened to Polish youths much sooner in life. He did appreciate the long life of his parents and for surviving the struggles they had for so many years just to live.

CHAPTER 34

WORKING AT WRIGLEYS

I'm going to retire," announced Ted Kolodziejski the following spring.

While Ted was much older than Wally, he assumed that people worked until they were really old before slowing down.

"You are retiring? How old are you, Ted?" Wally asked.

"I'm almost 65 now and Wrigley has a policy that you should retire at that age," he responded. And that was that.

Within a few weeks, it became official. There was a small party for Ted, and Mr. Wrigley attended. Wally wondered who his new boss would be.

The following day Wally was told to report to a man who controlled most of the work on the 17th floor. "Sit down, Wally," he said. "We have decided that you are the right person to be the manager of the supply room staff. You will take Ted's place starting today."

Wally was stunned. He remembered the other time that he was put in charge as a foreman in the coal mines so many years ago. He was apprehensive about this promotion. There was more pay but the same hours. Would it end as the other promotion? Would his coworkers respect him and this decision?

The following day he announced his new position to the other four members of the staff. To his amazement, no one said a word nor seemed surprised. Wally supervised this department for the rest of his career with Wrigley.

Along with his promotion, Wally gained a closer relationship with P.K. Wrigley. His son, Bill Wrigley, was now on board and helping to run much of the operations, but P.K. stayed with his beloved Cubs.

Once, he shared with Wally that in the late 1930s, he decided to plant Chinese elm trees in center field. They eventually blew down and Wrigley's front-office chose to replace the trees with ivy on the outfield walls. Those ivy covered walls were to last for more than 80 years and are still there.

Under P.K., Wrigley Field was the first major league baseball park to install an organ, the first to broadcast games live on the radio, and one of the first to televise them. The Cubs joined a partnership with WGN

TV, a relationship that developed into a superstation and made the Cubs one of America's favorite sports team.

But P.K., as much as he loved the Cubs and the ballpark, became reclusive as the years went by. There was a growing distance between him and his players. P.K. took less of an active role at Wrigley. His wife was extremely ill and still in a coma. P.K. was even lonelier.

Time quickly passed. Wally Jr. was growing and now attending grade school in the Wentworth area at the Holy Rosary Slovak Catholic School. The neighborhood continued to change for the worse. There seemed to be a steady movement of old neighbors out of the area. Then in 1969 there was a burglary.

One Friday night, Wally and Mary were returning home with young Wally from church, where he was an altar boy. They immediately noticed that there was a broken window near the front door. Then they heard noises from the back of the house and realized that the burglars were exiting as they were entering. The family lost watches, jewelry and even some money they had tucked in a drawer.

Wally Jr.'s piggy bank was smashed and Chippie, the family dog, had been beaten and locked in a bedroom. The family felt violated. They talked about what to do with the new crimes and unrest in the neighborhood. Their first move was to fortify the house. The windows were affixed with dowel rods so they couldn't be opened from the outside. A four by four piece of wood was propped against the door to prohibit it from being forced open. This was no way to live.

Then, brother-in-law Jim solidified the Pieszka/Abbeduto position. It was time for all of them to consider a move. Wally was convinced, too. The neighborhood had declined.

The Pieszka family began to look for a new location and was able to find an affordable home in the community of Hazel Crest. They moved in November of 1969.

It was harder for Mary to leave their original home. The memories, both sad and happy, were constantly on the minds of the family as they packed their belongings to move to a new community. This was their home when each child had been born. This was the neighborhood of Wally Jr.'s first school. Wally, however, was convincing to the family. Bad people were moving in as good people were moving out.

Not long after the Pieszka move, the entire Abbeduto family followed suit moving from the Wentworth community. Mr. Abbeduto died earlier that year, and Jim convinced his mother to leave the community that they had so loved. Wentworth had been a beautiful place to live for many years. But those times were over.

Mrs. Abbeduto and Jim also moved to Hazel Crest. Pat chose Oak Forest and Louie relocated in Chicago Heights. The entire family had moved away from their beloved community.

In 1970, while Wally was pushing a cart filled with IBM cards between floors, the doors opened, but the elevator was not flush with the floor. Wally, unaware of the height difference, pushed the cart into the edge. When it came to a sudden stop he struck his right knee on the back of the cart.

The pain was immediate. There was no choice but to go to a hospital. Wally was taken to one near his home and was seen by his family doctor.

"You have something in that knee, Wally. The X-ray shows it to be metallic. You are going to have to see a surgeon."

With that, he was taken to a room and was soon visited by another doctor, this one the surgeon. He was told he would have to wait a week for the swelling go down. There was to be no work until a further exam was done.

Wally waited the week at home in considerable pain, but the swelling did reduce some and Wally returned to the surgeon.

"Mr. Pieszka, you seem to have something lodged in your knee and it is interfering with the knee bending. Do you have any idea how this happened?"

It did not take Wally long to explain the appearance of metal in his leg. It was Stalingrad and the shrapnel. Apparently, they didn't get it all in either surgery during the war. The jolt from the cart must have moved this remaining piece.

The following day, surgery was performed. Mary and Wally Jr. both came to the hospital. Wally was not released from the hospital for ten days, with a bandaged knee and some real restrictions.

When the anesthetic wore off, Wally made a sad realization. The metal piece had not been saved. He thought that it would have been nice to have to remind him about how good life was compared to the day that piece of metal entered his leg so many years before.

Recovery was slow. Wally did not go back to work for almost three months. He was soon invited into P.K.'s office where he related the latest of his adventures. Perhaps now the last of Stalingrad would be gone.

Wally Jr. started attending the local public grade school, having transferred in the middle of fourth grade. The years passed and high school soon followed for young Wally. While he had little interest in sports, he enjoyed art and music. First, there was the guitar and then a chance to play on occasion with several bands. His hair grew long and shaggy, to the chagrin of his father. There were words, but the son prevailed, often with the argument that his father, as a Pole, just didn't understand the youth of America.

Mary continued working part-time with Mr. Levin and Wally continued as supervisor of the supply part of Wrigley's executive floor, both with a longer commute.

In the spring of 1977, word came down that P.K. was quite ill. His wife had passed away a year earlier and the man seemed to lose that last bit of vivacity Wally had come to know in those earlier years.

On April 12,1977, P.K. Wrigley died. The entire office was in mourning. P.K. was revered as a boss. His son, Bill, had been running the company for the last several years and Wally had attended to his needs.

It was never the same. The Wrigley Company was changing.

In 1981, Bill Wrigley sold the Chicago Cubs to the Tribune Company. The newspaper offices were just across Michigan Avenue from the Wrigley Building. It was thought that the Cubs were sold to generate the funds necessary to pay the incredible estate tax bills incurred by the deaths of Mrs. Wrigley and P.K. within such a short period of time.

During P.K.'s reign over the Cubs, they won 3,405 games and lost 3,631. They won the National League pennant in 1932, 1935, 1938 and 1945, but never won the World Series during Wrigley's ownership.

There was a long-standing joke that P.K. once shared facetiously in 1966: "They still do play the World Series, don't they? It's been so long, I don't remember."

The legacy of William Wrigley and his son, P.K., was over. There seemed to be a change of tone in the office. Wrigley was still the leader in chewing gum, but the atmosphere was different.

Still, Wally had never had a better job. Wally Jr. was finishing high school and talking of college. Wally needed to stay where he was.

CHAPTER 35

A SECOND TRIP TO POLAND

His son's high school graduation was a big deal for Wally. He himself never completed eighth grade, let alone 12 years of school. Wally was proud. In the spring of 1978, the entire Pieszka and Abbeduto families were going to the graduation ceremony. Wally Jr.'s grades were good and he was eligible for college. While his folks had not even visited a college, they relied on their son to make a wise choice.

There were two occasions on the horizon. The first was to properly celebrate Wally Jr.'s high school success. Second was a long awaited return to Poland for Wally. This time, he and Mary had saved enough money to go together. They also wanted to bring their son as a graduation present and give him a chance see his father's roots. Wally Jr. was not so sure that this should be his June 1978 summer plan.

Wally Jr. had worked enough at various odd jobs after school and in the summers to buy his own car, a used Dodge Charger. He also had a girlfriend. He occasionally played guitar in various local bands, and his hair had now grown past his shoulders. His dad still wasn't pleased and told him that he had to cut a least a foot off his hair off before any such trip. He finally consented, got the haircut, and packed his very American clothes, mostly Levis and sweatshirts. He also packed his cassette player and tapes.

Graduation went smoothly with a family party at the Abbeduto house after the ceremony. Comments were made about the "new" look being sported by the honoree, but Wally Jr. just smiled and accepted it. He was sure his band mates were laughing. They weren't going to Poland, however. Wally Jr. was getting excited.

Tickets were purchased and all had valid American passports along with visas for entering a communist country. They would be flying from Chicago's O'Hare airport on a Russian jet. There would be a stop at Goose Bay, Greenland, and then on to Warsaw.

It was going to be a different trip for Wally Sr. since his parents were now deceased. His house was now the home of Emil. They were to stay with Emil and his family. Fortunately, all of his brothers and their wives were alive and ready to host the American family. Frank and Andrew still lived within five or six miles of Emil.

177

The flight went smoothly. Young Wally marveled at the stop in Greenland. None of his friends had been outside the United States, let alone Greenland. There would be stories to tell.

Finally, the plane touched down in Warsaw. Customs took a bit of time. There outside the gate stood Frank, Emil, Andrew, their children and their wives, ten people in all. The three men now had three automobiles and easily packed away the visitors and their luggage. A big change since the last visit.

As he was driven out of Warsaw, Wally was surprised at the very few changes in the country since his last visit. It seemed to him that progress was not a large priority in the communist satellite country. Roads were rough, buildings still old, and while his brothers had cars, personal property was still scarce.

As the families talked over the days, the American family learned many things about living in present day Poland. It seemed that people were still not hard working. If one lost a job, he was told of his new one and the pay was always the same. Consequently, no one strived for better things in life. Unlike much of old Russia, Poland allowed people such as Emil to continue to own their own homes if they had them, but there was little else to purchase.

Mary was quickly unhappy. She loved the natural beauty of this country, but she only knew a few Polish words. As such, she could not participate in the many conversations. She patiently sat and pretended to listen. Often her mind wandered, hoping that sightseeing would soon follow. She later mentioned to Wally how long these family conversations lasted.

Wally Jr., on the other hand, had learned some Polish words and spoke a bit of German. The Polish family all spoke German. Wally Jr. quickly teamed up with the brothers' children, Angie, Janek and Joseph. They were eager to show their cousin the teenage life of Poland.

On more than a few occasions, the youngsters left their parents, bought vodka in the village and hiked into the woods. There they built campfires and spent the evenings drinking and telling stories about their lives in two totally different societies. Wally played cassettes on his player. His cousins eyed with envy this machine and the Levis that their American cousin wore every day.

At the time, tourists paid a head tax of $5 per person for each day they were in the country. While there were a few things one could buy, and while foreigners were allowed to bring money in, they were not permitted to take items and money out of the country. Wally Sr. bought a pergina comforter and two pictures that he was able to put in his luggage and bring home. Those were the only purchases that left Poland.

The sightseeing began in earnest the third day. The family toured on different days with different brothers. They saw Wally's school and his church. They drove to the fabled resort and restaurant of Zakopane in the mountains, the very mountains Wally had planned to hide in before talking to the priest about being drafted. They were more majestic and breathtaking when viewed as a forest rather than as an escape refuge.

Emil's wife, Sofia, cooked almost all the meals. Polish people in rural areas seldom ate in a restaurant. This was an added expense and the food was generally quite tasteless. Wally pondered this, having experienced so many good restaurants with different cuisines over the last 20 years.

On one such occasion preceding the meal at Sofia's table, a rather drunk man showed up on a motor scooter with three large knives. He was there to butcher a pig that Emil had behind the house. The man attacked the pig with a vengeance and soon was covered with blood, but the butchering was a success. The pig was roasted that evening, and some of the meat was saved and later made into sausage. None of the sausage was ready for the Pieszkas, as it wasn't finished curing by the time they left, but the cooking of the pig that evening sated the largest of appetites.

Wally missed his brothers, especially Andrew, and was pleased at seeing his niece and nephews. He missed aspects of his homeland but still had no desire to live there.

Life was simpler than his life in Chicago and at Wrigley's, and the people here did seem less stressed. They seemed to be more involved with the home and family life than their occupation. In most cases, having totally different jobs still paid the same. This was so not American. A laborer making the same wage as a craftsman or even a doctor did not make sense to Wally after his years of working in his new country.

The trip was over before the family could blink. The clothes were packed and the few purchased remembrances were half hidden among the suitcases.

Once again, the entire family transported the Pieszkas to Warsaw. As the airplane was loaded and last goodbyes were waved, Wally's thoughts turned to his life and being away from all of his family. Were it not for the abounding love of the Abbeduto family, life in America could have been long and arduous.

In spite of the warmth given to him by Mary's family, Wally felt a loss for his blood family. That was not enough for him to change countries after all this time. Years later, he marveled at the fact that his friends, the Zalases, wanted to return to their country of origin.

The flight back went smoothly with the same stop. This time they flew with the sun and not against it. The family arrived the same day they had left with their internal clocks completely confused.

Both Wally and Mary had planned to spend a couple of days recuperating before returning to work. Young Wally, however, was off to see his Dodge, his band friends and his girlfriend immediately.

Wally Jr. had seen enough. He had no desire to go back to Poland. While he thoroughly enjoyed the trip and the new experiences, he was an American, and the youth of America had no better time in history than the 1970s. Besides, college was ahead in September. He could let his hair grow if he wanted. He had ideas of a major but wasn't sure of a direction. Maybe the law or perhaps business. Time would tell.

That fall, Wally Jr. enrolled at Thornton Junior College, where he studied business. After two years, he transferred to Eastern Illinois University in Charleston, Illinois, a small city in central Illinois. During the summers, he worked at K-Mart and later got a summer job with his father's employer, Wrigley.

After graduation from college, Wally Jr. attended the Chicago Art Institute. He had always loved the arts and music, but after a short time he realized that there was no money in such a career and he went the business route. First, he worked for a company called Graphic Alliance, but soon after getting that job, the owner apparently absconded with all the money and one of the secretaries. When the place closed, Wally Jr. returned to Wrigley in 1981.

While beginning this working relationship with Wrigley, Wally Jr.'s life took the typical American twist, as the young guitarist/rocker met his wife, Lauren. They were married on September 14, 1985. They had two children, Debra in 1987 and Daniel in 1997. His father's lineage was to continue.

CHAPTER 36

BRINGING FAMILY TO AMERICA

In early 1979, Frank Kadzielnik and Wally started a conversation by letter. Would it be possible for Frank's daughter, Anelka, or Angie as she became known, to come to America and stay with her uncle?

It was now possible for a Polish person to get the papers to make a visit outside the country. U.S. customs could allow a person a temporary visa for six months.

In early May, Angie arrived at O'Hare International Airport. Wally and his family met her there. Her English was not very good, but with Wally's help she could converse. With Wally Jr. now attending college, there was room in the Hazel Crest house for the new visitor. Angie was 22 and had an associates degree in nursing, equivalent to a nurse with a two year degree here in the U.S.

Angie indicated that she wanted to work and earn some money before going back to Poland. There was a restaurant in Homewood, a small town nearby, owned by a Polish family called Surmas. Angie had no Social Security number, although that didn't seem to be a problem.

She started as a dishwasher and soon became a salad maker. In spite of the six-month limitation, Angie managed to stay with her uncle for the next two years. Her visitor visa was renewed several times, but Aunt Mary eventually received papers that it was time for Angie to go back to Poland.

During those two years, Angie studied English through a program given by Wrigley that Wally arranged. She had also met a young man named Charles Kmetz who had done carpentry work for her uncle. They saw each other a few times before December. In late December, 1980, the notice was received that she had to leave the country in seven days.

There was only one way to solve this problem. She didn't qualify as a student or as a political refugee. She had to get married. Whether for love or necessity, in early 1981, Angie married Charles Kmetz.

She asked Wally his opinion on whether she should marry so quickly, but he would not give one. He was not her father. So before the marriage, since letters were slow and irregular and no one in Poland had telephones in their homes, a phone call was arranged from an office in Chybie to Angie at Wally's house. Support for a wedding was not there.

Her parents begged her to come home. Her mother cried, but Angie was determined to be an American.

In February, having delayed the deportation with the help of a Wrigley attorney, Angie was married. The Catholic church demanded six months notice for a wedding, and the government would wait no more, so the couple was married in a civil ceremony by a judge in Cook County.

Early the following summer, Wally walked his niece down the aisle of St. Emeric's Church in Country Club Hills. The wedding reception was held at Surmas with many of her fellow workers in attendance. The marriage was now complete, according to the church, so Angie was safely a resident of the United States.

Angie's life in America continued with fairly menial jobs through the birth of her first two children: Anne in 1982 and Margaret in 1986.

When Margaret was born with a congenital cardiac problem, Angie decided to study this medical condition. Her studies brought her back to nursing and she became an assistant in the cardiology department of a neighborhood hospital. She had one more child, a son, Nicholas, in 1994.

Shortly after her marriage, her cousin Janek, or John as he was later called in America, expressed a desire to do what Angie had done. With the help of Wally, John came to Chicago in late 1982. He spent a year living at both the Pieszka home and Angie's house, working at Surmas as did his cousin. His English became quite good. At the end of a year, however, John decided to return to Poland.

During that year Wally's brother, Frank and his wife, Milka, made a trip to the U.S. to see their daughter and nephew. Frank stayed with Wally for several weeks before returning home. He was the only brother to come to America.

Wally was pleased that his niece decided to stay, as he always relished the company of family. As he aged, family became more important than ever. His son by now had given him two grandchildren, a daughter, Debra, and then a son, Danny.

Wally's life was good, but he realized that he was getting older. The next step was probably retirement when he was ready.

CHAPTER 37

RETIREMENT

It was 1986. Another year with the Wrigley Company was over. Wally was 63 and Mary was almost 66. Wally Jr. had spoken to his father about retirement for some time now.

In America, there seemed to be something magic about turning 65. Here, people expected a life-altering change at this magic age. Not so in Poland. There, people worked because they had to work. There were no retirement plans. There was no Social Security as such. Medical care in the Soviet Bloc was there if one could find it, but there was never any extra money to save for a retirement.

Wally's brothers had shared with him the good and the bad of living under a Communist regime. No one was yet aware of Glasnost, the Russian peace offering between President Reagan and Premier Gorbachev. While Wally and Mary had no specific plans for where they might retire, Poland was never in consideration after their earlier trip. Besides, a new task had arisen.

After Mary's father died in 1969, Jim became the principal support for his mother. Jim and Mrs. Abbeduto had moved to Hazel Crest and both families now lived in close proximity to each other. In 1986, Mrs. Abbeduto became quite ill. The primary care-giver was her son, Jim, but Wally and Mary joined in as needed. Mrs. Abbeduto often had told Wally that he was every bit her son.

The last several weeks of her life, Wally and Mary were with her at all times. Wally felt that he would care for her as he would have his own mother, had he had the chance.

He had never had that chance because of the distance and the rules of the now Communistic ways of Poland. The last weeks of Mrs. Abbeduto's life were in the hospital, and in 1988 Wally's "second mother" passed away. Jim then moved to the village of Beecher, and later to Tinley Park. The Hazel Crest house needed to be sold.

Wally was well aware that the sale of his mother-in-law's house in Hazel Crest would not be an easy task. At first, there were no offers. Later, there were a few, at a substantially reduced price. The family decided to take one of the offers and move on. Wally knew his home was depreciating just as Mary's mother's had. Hazel Crest had changed just as Roseland and Wentworth had changed. Good people were moving out, not in.

Now there were even fewer ties with the neighborhood in Hazel Crest. When Mrs. Abbeduto passed away, the reasons for staying employed and living in this area became even less significant. Crime was on the rise and the unemployed population grew. Sales were at give-away prices. First, it was Roseland, then Wentworth where their home was burglarized -- and now, Hazel Crest had police officers in the hallways of the high school.

Wally announced to Wrigley in May of 1989 that he wanted to retire. Their response was that he was a necessary cog in the business and knew so much after all this time, so could he not give them a couple of more years and train one of his workers to take over his job? While it was very flattering, Wally had enough. He told his employers that he would be leaving right after his birthday of May 23, his 65th birthday.

Since his son had been in grade school, Wally worked Saturdays and, on occasion, even a few Sundays. His life was his family and his work. Now his son was grown and living on his own.

As the date for retirement approached, Wally wondered if he should extend. But it was too late. Wrigley was going to throw a retirement party for this long-time employee.

The party took place on the 17th floor one Friday afternoon in late May, 1989. The room was large and was packed with people who had come to know Wally over the years. Of course, many of his old co-workers had since retired, but a handful of these retired men and women came to the party.

The principal speaker with kind remarks was none other than Bill Wrigley Jr. himself. Wally had personally tended to Bill's needs, as he had for his grandfather, P.K., and for Bill Sr. after that. Now it was the third generation. There was a large poster board present and all of the attendees signed their names and gave their well wishes. In the very center was the signature of Bill Wrigley.

That summer was spent around the house. There were a few things that needed to be fixed before the Pieszkas placed the house on the market. It was time.

On more than a few occasions, dinner was eaten with discussions of their next move. Wally Jr., now married, also had moved to Hazel Crest. Living so close allowed extra time with the entire family. As their only son, proximity was a definite consideration in where each family lived.

There were even a few evenings spent talking about Polish immigrants who had gone back to Poland after retiring from their American jobs. The Pregnitz family made such a move several years later to Belgium, and his friends, the Zalas family, later went back to Poland after Glasnost.

That summer, the decision was made to put the Hazel Crest home on the market. It was listed with a competent realtor, but there was little interest.

In October, the first real interest was shown by an African-American woman. She wanted a house for herself and was interested in leaving the south side of Chicago. She offered only $38,000, well below what Wally believed it was worth. However, other offers were non-existent.

They were ready to accept the price when the woman added one more stipulation. She wanted possession in two weeks!

Mary hesitated in agreeing to the sale. This area had been her family neighborhood for 20 years. Her brothers lived fairly close by, and Wally Jr. was not far off. Where were they to go? Who would be her new friends?

All of these thought filled Mary's head each day. Wally agreed to keep the move close to the city of Chicago, but where?

Down deep, Mary also knew that they needed to move, and finally she consented to the sale.

The contract was signed on a Friday and the hunt for a place to live started in earnest. Could they find a place? Did they need to find an apartment as they looked?

And then a realtor from Bourbonnais, Illinois, appeared like a saint.

After visiting their son and family at his home one Sunday, Wally and Mary ventured south to Bourbonnais, a small village attached to the north side of Kankakee. They wandered into a real estate office and met a realtor named Shirley St. Germaine. She was working that Sunday and wasted no time. They were in her car and driving through the neighborhoods of Bourbonnais, Bradley and Kankakee almost immediately.

They shared their dilemma of immediacy with her, and Mrs. St. Germaine had a new thought. She headed out of the towns and into the countryside. She knew of an empty house that was part of a farm. It was readily available, because the mother of the farmer with the land surrounding the house had died. The woman had been living by herself in the house and it could be sold separately from the rest of the farm.

Wally fell in love with the place, and Mary consented. It was a wreck, but it had potential. It came with four acres of property. The price was $93,000.

While it was a fair price, Wally and Mary had little money coming from the Hazel Crest home sale, but with the help of Mrs. St. Germaine, a short term loan was obtained and the closings took place just five days after the Hazel Crest contract was signed.

They had a home. But the lifestyle was going to be quite different.

185

Their mailing address was a village called Bonfield. Bonfield had no grocery store or gas station. It had fewer than 1,000 people. The village was also three miles from the new Pieszka home. Driving was to become a very necessary part of day-to-day living. And Mary did not drive any longer.

The move had to be done immediately. Both closings were done on the same day in Homewood, Illinois. But when the actual move was to take place, there was a problem. All of the moving companies had waiting lists and were not available. Wally Jr. had an idea. He knew a man with a large truck. With the help of the truck owner, Wally Jr.'s father-in-law, and Wally Jr., the entire move was done in two days, in spite of the many loads and 40-mile drive each way.

The house needed work. The first requirement was to find a hardware store or lumber yard. Wally found one immediately. Van Voorst Lumber was only a few miles away in Union Hill and had most of what he needed. A friendship developed over the years and the lumber yard often gave unused lumber to Wally for many of his woodworking projects.

The first of many Bonfield friendships had started. Wally was to learn that word of mouth was better than a telephone book in order to find solutions to everyday problems with the new rural living.

Their chimney developed problems. Across the road were three houses, one of which was that of Len Tetrault. The man repaired chimneys and he agreed to fix Wally's problem. Another friend was added. That friendship lasted until Len's death. Len was also a World War II veteran, and conversations often went on for hours as the two visited over the years.

Mary was a city girl. Wally had been raised a country boy. While he was quite comfortable in this rural setting, it was isolation to Mary. She needed a social life. The first step was in finding a church.

Mrs. St. Germaine once again entered the picture. Sacred Heart Catholic Church in Goodrich was nearby. Mrs. St. Germaine recommended this church as one that might fit with the Pieszkas. After several visits, they decided that this was the church for them.

Mary joined the women's group and was immediately accepted. Wally became a free maintenance man who cared for the grounds of the church. He also was a greeter each Sunday. He became quite close with the parish priest, Father Paul Jasinski. Both of the Pieszkas felt accepted into this friendly rural society. They rarely missed a Sunday Mass.

The transition had been made. Wally's life style had changed in so many ways over the years. This one was not about to cause him a problem. Eighteen years of rural farming, to a German military barracks and foreign places of war, then the coal mines of Scotland, to the city life near Oxford and the inner city of Chicago, followed by suburban life. Finally, it was a return to the rural farming setting that comforted Wally.

He was at peace with his lawn and home, his garden and fruit trees, his rural church and small-town friendships. His life had in many ways had gone a full circle.

The years that followed were the best years of Wally's life. He and Mary were a solid part of an accepting community. Their house became a home. The carpeting was replaced and woodwork redone. The kitchen was modernized and a new room was added to the rear of the house as a family room with stereo and television.

The outside was changed with the addition of a large garden which produced a number of vegetables, the favorite of which was a patch of rhubarb. A statue of the Virgin Mary was placed in the front of the house with flowers surrounding her. More trees were planted, including apple and pear. Mary came to love her new home.

Wally also started a new passion: woodworking. He made a number of household items that he distributed to friends in the community. He had a favorite project and that was a bird on a metal post. The bird's wings were separate pieces of wood that turned with the wind. The bird also pivoted around the post that was planted in the ground so that the bird always faced the wind much like a weather vane. The flapping bird caused much consternation with other birds and some animals who attempted to invade Wally's garden. Soon there was a "market" for the device and Wally freely handed out these "scarecrows" to his neighbors and friends.

Weekends often found Wally Jr. and his family visiting the rural home for Sunday meals or Saturday get-togethers. The new millennium came and went, but the lives of Wally and Mary stayed fairly consistent.

As with all things in life, shortly after the new century arrived, the life of Wally Pieszka would again change.

CHAPTER 38

THE LAST TRIP BACK

In 1994, Wally developed a certain longing to once again visit his country of birth.

The changes in Poland and its political structure were world news. Communism was dying and Russia was losing its grip on the Soviet Union's border countries. He had to see it for himself.

There were many conversations with Mary. She really did not want to go. She spoke no Polish. She always felt accepted but not included when they visited Wally's family in 1978. She agreed that they could afford a trip for one, and in her own subtle way, excluded herself from the trip. Wally would visit alone for one month.

This time, the flight was more direct since international relations had eased considerably. Again, Wally was able to join a tour group with no requirement to travel with the group once they arrived in Poland. This kept the price fairly reasonable.

Wally arrived in Warsaw. Emil, Andrew and Frank met him at the airport. The change was evident as soon as he exited the aircraft. There was little security and no soldiers with weapons. The roads had asphalt, even to Ilownica. As the family drove to there, the conversation flowed. All the brothers talked openly. The threat of the government watching and controlling life seemed to have disappeared.

So far, however, many physical aspects of the country had not improved. The few new buildings were bleak and without character. Andrew explained that while the freedom was there, the money was not, as the Soviet Union had, for all practical purposes, gone bankrupt.

Poland was not far from the same economic fate. All money that had flowed from Moscow to Poland had ceased. Just like East Germany, Moscow was no longer in a position to provide economic or military aid, and the infamous Wall had fallen. Clearly, Poland was on its own. The long term hope was to join the European Union.

Wally again stayed in Emil's home. Janek, his son, had moved to Bielsko and had a good job. Fortunately, the advice given to their mother about the transfer of ownership to Emil was correct, and had Wally not ceded his rights as an heir, the home could have been lost when his mother died.

As the visit continued and Wally was driven around, changes did become noticeable. More people had cars, shops and stores had more merchandise, and ownership was now available on everything.

Emil, with the help of money sent to him by Wally, was able to buy the business for which he had worked and he now had his own automotive repair shop.

The month sped by. It was good to see his brothers and especially his nephew Janek, who had lived with him for a year in the United States. His English was still good and he had married a wonderful woman. It seemed that the year had broadened his understanding of the business world and was helping him in his new job.

It was with sadness that the goodbyes were said. Within the next few years, all of his brothers would die without seeing Wally again. The four of them posed for a picture that last week, a photograph that Wally would treasure.

Upon the death of Emil, Janek inherited the family home, now having been in the Pieszka/Kadzielnik name since 1927. It was pleasing to Wally that Janek inherited it. Family traditions should go on, and this home was always the gathering place for the family on holidays and get-togethers.

Wally could fly home, pleased with his Polish family and with his decisions. Down deep, Wally knew he would not return to his homeland.

CHAPTER 39

THE DEATH OF MARY

The summer of 2003 was going to be long and hot. The corn was growing on three sides of the Pieszka rural home in Bonfield. There were visits by friends, fellow church-goers, and Wally Jr.'s family, but most days were spent inside with just the two of them.

Mary had been complaining of not feeling well for some time, but she never was one to overly state her health problems. However, now she knew something was wrong.

Over the weekend, Wally, Mary and Wally Jr.'s family visited Angie. As Mary sat quietly in a chair, it was clear to all that her face was gray. Wally and Mary returned home that night, but it was clear Mary needed to see her doctor.

The next morning, an appointment was made with Dr. Phillip Hays, and the couple drove to his office. Dr. Hays ordered some tests and told the couple to return home. By the time they reached Bonfield, there was a message to return to the hospital.

As was his custom, Dr. Hays met the family at the emergency room. Apparently, the tests were back and Wally could see the concern on Dr. Hays's face. Mary was to stay in the hospital. She was transfused with five units of blood and prescribed a drug called Procrit. This drug was to help her body produce blood.

"I am referring you to Dr. Mehmet Sipahi," Dr. Hays began. He gently explained that this doctor was a cancer specialist.

Both Mary and Wally caught their breaths as more was explained to them.

The tests had indicated more than a problem with Mary's blood. Some rather complicated terms were used. The doctor explained that it was not unlike leukemia, a cancer of the blood.

The appointment was arranged and the couple went home with the fear that hangs over any family that has just heard the word cancer used about a loved one.

Dr. Sipahi saw the couple within a few days and again repeated the diagnosis. He explained that the blood disorder came from a cancer in Mary's bone marrow, the place where new blood is made. Mary was not making blood in the amounts necessary for her to stay healthy.

Dr. Sipahi informed them that there would be a need for blood transfusions on occasion in order to keep Mary as healthy as possible. He did not say that there was a cure as such, but recommended that some treatments begin as soon as possible.

When asked about these treatments, the doctor responded that the cost could well exceed $10,000 for the Pieszka family. When Wally privately asked what the chances of survival were, the doctor grimly told him that they could expect no more than a year even with these drugs. Wally decided not to share this with Mary. Wally and Mary declined these extra treatments and chose a conservative approach with medication for pain.

These conservative measures were begun within a week. More tests were run. Injections were given. On some occasions, Mary was infused with blood, but she seemed to weaken steadily. A decision was made to bring in Hospice of Kankakee. They provided various supplies and a hospital bed that was put into the marital bedroom. Wally often slept a few hours on the couch in the living room. He sat with her constantly. When he went to church, he prayed, as a friend sat with his wife.

While Hospice came twice a week, the community would provide additional care for Mary. A friend from church, Terry Weakly, stepped in. She organized church women to assist Wally. Wally and Mary could still go out on occasion, especially to church on Sundays, but trips were limited.

Soon the entire parish in Goodrich knew of her plight. His history and plight through the war was now well known, and he was a favorite at his church, Sacred Heart of Goodrich. Mary was popular with the women of the church as well.

The days were long but the weeks flew by. Wally was losing weight and could never seem to get much sleep. For a while, Mary would be taken to the doctor's office, but after a few trips she just couldn't make the car rides. Nurses came from Riverside Hospital in Kankakee every second day. Medication was now just for the pain.

By April of 2004, church women were spending the night, sleeping in the guest room and answering Mary's needs through the night, allowing Wally some sleep. Later that month, Mary spent a few days in the hospital but returned home.

Wally and his son sat for hours with this beloved wife and mother. Wally often talked of his and Mary's early years, remembering details of their meeting, this Italian woman and Polish man. He recalled how Mary's family had taken Wally in like a son.

Wally thought of being with his mother-in-law during her last days in the hospital, saying to him, "Wally, I am going to get out of here and bake you your favorite bread." That did not happen.

Perhaps those last days in the hospital for Mrs. Abbeduto led to the determination of Wally and Mary to have these last months in their home.

Just before midnight on May 11, 2004, Wally knew the end was near. While his son was in the other room getting some well-deserved rest, Wally sat by his wife and just held her. Suddenly, there was a loud gasp and Mary sagged in his arms. There was nothing more he could do.

His son made a call to the ambulance personnel. They arrived shortly and pronounced Mary dead. Schreffler's Funeral Home was called and by 2:00 a.m., a hearse had arrived and her body had been removed with her official date of death on May 12. Funeral arrangements had been made long ago for both of them with Schreffler's in Kankakee.

There was a whirlwind of activity, mostly handled by the women of the parish. There was a wake at the funeral home that Thursday night. The crowd just did not quit. This transplanted couple had become very special to their community.

It bothered Wally that their long-time priest, Father Paul Jasinski, had passed away. There would be a new priest conducting the services in the Goodrich church.

Since Father Jasinski had been ill for some time, a temporary priest had been assisting the parish. Wally knew him but not as well as his regular priest. Wally had gone to Sunday 7:30 a.m. Mass at the church without fail for two years. He had cared for all the outside flowers for years.

While he and Mary had been members of this church since moving to Bonfield, he never served on a church board or any committee. He talked little about his World War II experiences, since that would exclude Mary from the conversations.

Wally had become a better listener over the years. Perhaps that was maturity or a greater respect for his wife.

The funeral was on Friday. The services were in the family church. The pallbearers were nephews, Keith and Dennis Abbeduto, and husbands of nieces, Charles Kmetz and David Beveridge, along with one church member, David Park. A sixth pallbearer was one of the funeral personnel. The service included a Mass, and the church was filled.

The cemetery, Mt. Hope, is two miles south of the church, surrounded by fertile Illinois farmland. The headstone was previously purchased and placed at the head of the grave. Wally and Mary had their names engraved. The dates of death were to be added later. There were two angels affixed to the top of the tombstone, one from the women of the church and one from Wally.

They stood over the graves with cherubic faces. Not far away was the grave of Father Jasinski. As Wally watched the final rites, he realized the finality of death. He had seen death in gruesome forms since his days at Auschwitz and Stalingrad. He thought of the piles of frozen German and Russian soldiers stacked in Stalingrad in December of 1942.

Those thoughts gave him some solace. Here in the quiet corn fields of central Illinois, there was dignity in death and respect for the departed.

After the burial, there was a dinner back at the church hall. Again, the hall was packed. Mary's three surviving brothers, Pat, Jim and Louie, were there with their families.

A meal was served and the guests left. Many stopped by that afternoon as Wally and his son hosted the friends and family.

Then they all went home, including his son and family.

He was alone -- really alone.

Over the next few days, Wally packed up all of Mary's clothing and many of her books and personal things to deliver them to a Catholic charity in Kankakee. Perhaps having fewer items of hers around the home would help ease the loneliness.

CHAPTER 40

LIFE IN BONFIELD

At first, the days passed slowly. The rural setting in the farm community surrounding a small Midwest village was peaceful but lonely. The daily conversation with Mary was painfully missing. Giving her clothing away hadn't helped. The entire home was a reminder of her.

Wally decided that he must stay busy. It was the only way to survive this rural prison that had been their joy. After a few months, Wally attacked the house. He had neglected it rather badly for some time, as Mary's care took so much of each day.

He cleaned and moved furniture. He washed everything he could. He swept the garage again and again. His favorite tools in the garage became familiar friends again and he returned to creating wooden objects. His wooden birds with wings that rotated with the wind dominated his creative time. He made dozens of these painted protectors of the seeds, giving the wooden creatures to friends and fellow church goers.

Wally returned to the church. Every Sunday he was the principal greeter at the front door. The flowers and landscaping around the church were still his mission. The church members awaited his arrival and included him in all the local events.

In the growing seasons, Wally's garden produced far more crops than he could use. Often he brought tomatoes, peppers and other vegetables to friends and church members. His rhubarb patch exceeded expectations. He even found a purchaser of this bounty in Blue's Café, one of his favorite eating spots and the maker of the best pies in the Kankakee area.

Wally tried to reconnect with old friends when possible. The Pregnitz family had left the United States, moving to Belgium. He had written contact with them for a while, but both died a few years after Mary.

Wally's old world was shrinking.

Wally Jr.'s life was busy with two children and a full time job at Wrigley's. His daughter had finished college by this time. His son continued to reside with his parents at home. His visits to his father were as frequent as possible.

For Wally Sr., the days between the weekends had to be filled. He still did all of his own yard work, in spite of approaching and reaching his 90s. He mowed his own grass, trimmed his many trees, planted and harvested his own fruit and vegetables. His reflexes allowed him to retain his driver's license year after year, often to the surprise of the examiner.

In 2011, while visiting Dr. Hays to deliver a Christmas present, he was introduced to another of the doctor's patients. But this one was a bit different. He was a local lawyer who began writing a weekly column in the *Daily Journal,* a Kankakee newspaper. They talked, and Wally was asked if he would allow his story to be shared in an article in that newspaper. No one had ever asked him to reveal his story for the purpose of recording his incredible life. With some hesitation, he consented.

That spring, three full pages of the newspaper shared his life with local readers. The response was great. The local church members saved their copies of the paper and brought them to him. He was now a bit of a local legend.

Then one day, Wally contacted the writer. "I did you the favor of sharing my life story with you. Now you must do me a favor."

The writer quickly agreed and was off to Bonfield. "We are going to the cemetery. I must show you something."

Wally and the writer got in the car and headed for the cemetery where his wife was buried. There on a slight hill was a magnificent monument with Mary's name, date of birth and date of death. Next to that was a space reserved for Wally's name and information.

"Look at the top of the monument. There used to be two angels on top. One I bought and the other was given by the ladies of our church," he said, with tears in his eyes. Someone had stolen the angels and defaced Wally's tribute to his beloved Mary.

"I want you to write an article about this terrible act. It is disgusting." The writer asked if there could be a part of the article that might deal with funds being raised to replace the angels, but Wally would have none of that. "I just want to shame the bad people who created this travesty."

The article was written and there was an outpouring of sympathy and offers of donations coming from different places, the longest distance being from a reader in Florida. Wally would not change his mind. There would be no replacement of the angels.

A friendship developed between Wally and the writer. "Your story is one of many about the cruelty of war, but it is unique in that the bad luck of life-threatening and life-changing events in each case had good luck prevail. Do you know how unique your story is? A man who wore both uniforms in the same war! I have recently read *Unbroken* by Laura Hillenbrand. Louie Zamperini has nothing on you. You need your own book."

It was explained to Wally that Zamperini was an Olympic athlete in the 1932 games in Berlin. He later became a crew member of a B-24 in the Pacific during World War II that crashed in the ocean. He survived more than 40 days afloat in a life raft, only to be rescued by the Japanese and horribly tortured as a prisoner of war.

And the project started. Weekly visits with copious note taking commenced. Wally seemed to enjoy the new company and related his life piece by piece. The writer, lacking the experience of writing a book, sought an author. A letter to the publisher of *Unbroken* resulted in a cordial response informing the writer that Mrs. Hillenbrand now suffered from chronic pain syndrome, no longer wrote, and virtually never left her house.

A chance meeting by the writer with an old college friend who had been one of the hostages in the American Embassy in Teheran, Iran, for 444 days resulted in another conversation for finding a qualified writer.

"I helped one writer with his book about our experiences in 1979. He wrote *Guests of the Ayatollah*, but is probably better known for his book *Blackhawk Down* about Somalia. His name is Mark Bowden. I will give him a call," the friend responded.

Mark Bowden did call the writer and expressed interest in such a book, but the lack of time prevented him from jumping in. "I am teaching 25 students at the University of Delaware and working on two books of my own. I can't do it. But you can. And it sounds like a best seller." He then spent almost an hour explaining how one could write his first book.

"Well, Wally. I guess it is up to us. Are you game to give this non-fiction book a run?" the writer asked. The relationship took on a totally new closeness. There were weekly visits in the dozens. The author took a trip to Poland to see the village of Ilownica, the built and rebuilt home of Wally's childhood, and the remaining members of the Kadzielnik family in order to try to grasp the geography and emotion of the Polish past.

Wally deserves the best book that could be written, but this is what he could get at 94 years of age. With his health deteriorating some, there was a rush to finish this endeavor. Hospital visits became more frequent in the spring of 2017. Driving his car came to an end, as well.

While age creeps up on him as this last chapter is being written, it is not the end. This survivor still survives. He would not quit for the pneumonia, the Germans, the Russians, the coal mines, the labor unions of Chicago, the pain of losing a daughter, nor the death of his wife.

We who have had the comfort and safety during wars in our own country can only partially understand what so many people in the world went through in those terrible years of World War I and World War II. Some people are private examples of determination.

Wally was the ultimate survivor from birth. Thankfully, he agreed to share his life of disasters and salvation, his near death experiences, heartbreaking events, and finally his chance to live a free and productive life in his chosen new country.

Wally Pieszka, an American.

The Ultimate Survivor

The Ultimate Survivor